AF255663

Wondrous in His Saints

Wondrous in His Saints

Essays to Inspire on the Orthodox Patristic Tradition

Chris Baghos

WIPF *&* STOCK · Eugene, Oregon

WONDROUS IN HIS SAINTS
Essays to Inspire on the Orthodox Patristic Tradition

Wipf & Stock
An Imprint of Wipf and Stock Publishers
199 W. 8th Ave., Suite 3
Eugene, OR 97401

www.wipfandstock.com

PAPERBACK ISBN: 978-1-6667-7341-5
HARDCOVER ISBN: 978-1-6667-7342-2
EBOOK ISBN: 978-1-6667-7343-9

06/20/23

For my wife and son, parents and wider family,
and past and present mentors.

May the church fathers intercede for you,
now and always and to the ages of ages.

God is wondrous in His saints;
The God of Israel shall give power
    and strength to His people.
Blessed is God.

—Psalm 67:36 (SAAS)

Contents

Introduction

The Fathers and Mothers of the Church
as Spiritual Guides

It is impossible to heal our spiritual infirmities without attempting to build an intimate relationship with the Lord Jesus Christ, in whose image and likeness we have been fashioned. In his altruistic compassion, the Lord has already offered us a remedy to all such afflictions via his assumption of our nature, his establishment of the new covenant by means of the Eucharist, his founding of the church through the apostles. Yet one cannot hope to know the Lord by reading certain books of the New Testament in isolation as certain Christian denominations espouse. We know that the Orthodox tradition preceded the composition of the gospels, not merely their compilation. More precisely, knowledge of the Lord and the customs which he established had been directly transmitted from holy elders to their disciples before the church was ever compelled to leave any records for posterity. The reasons for her eventual expression of the faith in writing need not worry us. What matters is that tradition was first embodied by certain people, namely those who made a genuine effort to interiorize Christ's commandments and imitate his lifestyle.

The Scriptures served as a means of ensuring the successful continuation of such imitation, though not alone. The Divine Liturgy, the Eucharist, and the remaining sacraments (e.g., baptism, holy unction, marriage, and ordination) were essential to the life of the church from her humble beginnings. With the passing of time, we had the convening of councils, the formulation of doctrines, the composition of canons. Moreover, the church developed her own art through icons and hymns while at the same time emphasizing the significance of personal prayer—especially the Jesus Prayer—for our spiritual transformation. Undeniably, our church preserves and develops these various aspects of the faith in obedience to our Lord Jesus Christ, from whom they ultimately proceed and to whom they finally direct us. She does so by appealing to the holy fathers and mothers, in whom Christ is revealed and to whom the various aspects of tradition are first entrusted.

There is an informal distinction on the part of the church between our local fathers (e.g., confessors, monks, and parish priests) and mothers (e.g., abbesses, nuns, and pious female elders) and those whom she universally celebrates as such because of their having attained the state of holiness. We call upon the latter fathers and mothers collectively at every liturgy, most famously in our concluding prayer (Δι' εὐχῶν τῶν ἁγίων Πατέρων ἡμῶν, Κύριε Ἰησοῦ Χριστὲ ὁ Θεός, ἐλέησον καὶ σῶσον ἡμᾶς).[1] We commemorate them individually on their respective feast days. They are depicted on the walls of every church, serving as our faithful companions during the celebration of each sacrament. The church, in her wisdom, has adopted terms that emphasize our unity as a family. We are called to recognize and embrace God's holy ones as our loving guardians, as examples of how we should live.

Certain Christian denominations appeal to the apparent prohibition of the term "Father" by the Lord in the gospels as a means of criticizing Orthodox, Roman Catholics, and Anglicans: e.g., "And call no one your father on earth, for you have one Father—the one in heaven" (Matt 23:9 NKJV). By recognizing the wisdom of past generations, however, we know how to correctly interpret this passage. To be sure, St Jerome of Stridon, a formidable exegete and theologian of the mid-fourth to early-fifth century, rushed to the defense of the monks of Palestine who had been questioned for reverently calling each other "fathers" by those who did not comprehend the nuances of Scripture. Having acquired discernment by means of ascetic effort, on the one hand, and training under spiritual leaders like St. Gregory the Theologian, on the other, Jerome affirmed that God the Father must lovingly be referred to as such with respect to his nature since he is our maker and master. He stated that our spiritual elders

---

1. *Divine Liturgy of Our Father Among the Saints John Chrysostom*, 110.

should be acknowledged as "fathers" and "mothers" not on account of any innate qualities but because the Lord himself has enabled them to make progress in the holy life. It is only fitting that we should show them reverence and affection by using such appellations, thus cultivating humility with a view to our salvation.[2]

There is an arbitrary categorization of the fathers and mothers on the part of scholarship which limits their existence to either the second century (the last of the "Apostolic Fathers," the immediate successors of the Lord's disciples) or the eighth century (the Second Council of Nicaea in 787). The church recognizes the "patristic" (from *pater, patris* in Latin, and πατήρ, πατρός in Greek) phenomenon as ongoing owing to its conviction that men and women throughout the ages have known Christ face to face. The church emphasizes that the saints have responded to the Lord's loving call through their obedience and self-denial, their affection towards him and all humankind. Always belonging to the ecclesiastical framework, they have become "little Christs" entrusted with its growth, preservation and, at certain times, admonition. It is noteworthy that the saints of the past are alive in Christ, joining those of today in their performance of such tasks.

From the fourth to sixth centuries, after the legalization of Christianity by St. Constantine the Great, many among the faithful still desired to imitate the early martyrs whom they believed shared in Christ's triumph over death because of their detachment from worldly interests. They subsequently ventured to the deserts of Egypt, Mesopotamia, and Asia Minor where they disciplined their bodies to strengthen their souls. Because of the physical and spiritual struggles that they encountered in the wilderness, these ascetics—both men and women—were highly revered by the church. It was believed that their prayers facilitated the welfare of the entire world, especially the cities. As indicated by St. Jerome, they often referred to their pious elders as either "father" (ἀββᾶ/ἀββᾶς) or "mother" (ἀμμά/ἀμμᾶς). The stories and sayings of these saints were eventually recorded by their disciples. Two collections survive (i.e., the alphabetical and the thematic). They remain an important source of guidance and consolation for us Orthodox Christians.

The two collections are largely complementary because of their depictions of men and women with the same existential goal, namely deification, and living encounter with Christ. Nevertheless, they attest to different spiritual practices and attitudes among the Greek, Egyptian, and Syriac monks

---

2. Jerome of Stridon, *Commentary on Matthew*, 260–61.

and nuns. This is especially evidenced by a certain story concerning Sts. Arsenius the Great and Moses the Ethiopian. In short, there was a monk who wished to visit Arsenius, a former teacher of the imperial family much admired for his ascetic rigor and spiritual fortitude. The monk, however, did not wish to stay long with Arsenius upon meeting him, uncomfortable with his silence and introversion. He therefore left immediately with the brother who had escorted him to the saint's cell. The monk then asked his brother to take him to Moses, a former thief who likely never received an education but nonetheless displayed much wisdom and grace. In contrast to Arsenius, Moses proved to be an enthusiastic and joyous host. The monk was compelled to confess his preference for the company of the Ethiopian. Another father soon heard this story and sought an explanation from God in prayer as to why the one ascetic should flee from men for his name's sake while the other should embrace them. "Then two large boats were shown to him on a river and he saw Abba Arsenius and the Spirit of God sailing in the one, in perfect peace; and in the other was Abba Moses with the angels of God, and they were all eating honey cakes."[3]

It is noteworthy that the means of travel and the location are the same for both saints despite their unique temperaments and ethnic and social backgrounds. The one has been granted profound peace, the other, overwhelming joy. The boats can be taken as an image of the ascetic life, the river, the kingdom of heaven. Indeed, it should not surprise us that very different holy men and women have cooperated throughout the ages for the benefit of the church. For instance, St. Athanasius of Alexandria, a hierarch well-versed in Greek rhetoric, enlisted the help of St. Antony the Great, a hermit with what was likely a very basic education, to refute the heretic Arius who denied the divinity of our Lord Jesus Christ by considering him a creature. Athanasius revered Antony for the wisdom that he had acquired through ascetic struggle. Antony respected Athanasius for his learning and status as a bishop.

Judging from the lives the saints, the Lord wants all of us to be saved regardless of our gender, ethnicity, upbringing, marital status, occupation, and level of education. He has therefore inspired men and women of various backgrounds, with different dispositions and interests, to imitate him. The church in turn promotes their memory for the sake of catechetical instruction and conversion in fulfilment of the Lord's command to make disciples of all peoples (Matt 28:18–20). It is important to note that the saints never

3. *Sayings of the Desert Fathers: The Alphabetical Collection,* 17–18.

criticized or condemned one another on account of their differences. The church is truly the one body of Christ with each member having their own unique function, as St. Paul tells us (1 Cor 12:12–27). Carrying this analogy further, the church features both unity and distinction like the very person of Christ, who is fully God and fully man. Our unity (not uniformity) is best evidenced by our saving confession, neatly articulated in the "Prayer of the Presentation" that we recite together during the liturgy: "Deacon: Let us love one another, that with one mind we may confess: / People: Father, Son and Holy Spirit, Trinity of one essence and inseparable."[4]

The church fathers and mothers occupy a central place within tradition. In cooperation with Christ, it is they who have: determined the canonical corpus of Scripture (e.g., St. Irenaeus of Lyons); interpreted it correctly on our behalf (e.g., St. John Chrysostom); composed the sacred songs of the church (e.g., Sts. Andrew of Crete and Kassiani the Hymnographer); structured the liturgy and outlined its meaning for our sake (e.g., Sts. Maximus the Confessor and Nicholas Kabasilas); given us the theological justification for the use of icons (e.g., Sts. John Damascene and Theodore the Studite); defended, comforted, and safeguarded the church during times of crisis (e.g., St. Mark of Ephesus). This is in addition to their formulation of doctrine and innumerable contributions to the church's understanding of the world, the human person, and the artistic creativity of humankind.

The church fathers and mothers demonstrate that we can all be saved if we respond to Christ's loving call. We may identify our own strengths and weaknesses, our hopes and fears, in them. They comfort and encourage us not only in their writings but through the examples of their lives. Is anyone we know struggling with the loss of a loved one? Let's point them to St. Gregory of Nyssa, who related in his treatise *On the Soul and the Resurrection* how he was comforted by his dying elder sister, St. Macrina the Younger, upon having lost their brother, St. Basil the Great.[5] Has any sister in Christ been belittled because of her gender? Let her remember Sts. Syncletica of Alexandria and Sarah of the Desert, who each proved wrong those that doubted their fortitude by becoming models of asceticism and spiritual luminaries. Is any parent being grieved by a disobedient child that has strayed from the church? Is any child struggling to return to the fold? Let's provide both parent and child with a copy of St. Augustine of Hippo's *Confessions*, in which the theologian relates how the Lord rewarded his pious

---

4. *Divine Liturgy*, 65.

5. Gregory of Nyssa, *On the Soul and the Resurrection*, 27.

mother Monica for her patience by compelling him to fully commit to the Christian life in his thirties with tears of compunction.[6] That such radical transformation is open to all is demonstrated by the *Life of St. Mary Egypt*, a prescribed reading for Lent. This hagiography describes how a naïve though very virtuous monk, St. Zosimas of Palestine, encountered a former harlot, Mary, in the desert and learned about her miraculous transformation into a "little Christ" through the intercession of the Theotokos.

Our forebears found the time to learn about the saints despite their countless physical hardships, lesser educations, and comparative lack of leisure. We must ask ourselves what is more important for our salvation: the latest updates on social media regarding the most recent political scandal, last night's football game, a highly anticipated film, or those proverbs, stories, and treatises that teach us how to pray, how to engage in asceticism, how to nurture the virtues? To this end, the present book highlights key teachings from, and existential examples of, apostles, ascetics, martyrs, and theologians belonging to a range of contexts across two millennia: from the formation and formal defense of the church in Late Antiquity to the prolific expansion of the faith in the West during the early medieval period, from the major monastic developments of Byzantium in the High Middle Ages to the resplendence and twilight of the Russian missions in the Far East during modernity.

The following chapters vary in scope, theme, and content, focusing especially on the saints' insights into intimate aspects of the spiritual life (including prayer, repentance, love, and deification), as well as their perceptions of the degree to which the faithful should engage with science and culture, on the one hand, and renounce the world during times of tyranny, on the other. The chapters have been arranged in loose chronological order, yet readers are welcome to dive directly into those topics which interest them. I do not pretend to offer any wisdom of my own in this work but to share and reiterate that which I have been privileged to discover from the church fathers and mothers over the course of my formal philosophical and theological studies at the University of Sydney and St Andrew's Greek Orthodox Theological College. The most important of these discoveries is, perhaps, the egalitarian nature of Orthodoxy, that the experience of holiness has never been restricted to any time, place, social class, or clerical rank but always attainable for men and women seeking communion with our Lord and Savior. Let us call on the holy fathers and mothers cited throughout

6. Augustine of Hippo, *Confessions*, 170–79.

this work—Jewish, Greek, Latin, Egyptian, Celtic, Anglo-Saxon, and Chinese—for their loving intercessions, that Christ, God the Son and master of all, may likewise reveal himself wondrous in us.

1

St. Peter as a Model of Repentance

THERE IS A MISCONCEPTION on the part of certain denominations that repentance simply consists in sorrow and guilt. There is, of course, an inherent danger in this mentality since it can lead to listlessness, self-loathing, and self-harm. On the other side of the spectrum, there are those who joyously proclaim that they are already "saved" whilst making very little effort to overcome their sinful habits. This attitude is synonymous with pride, an inflated ego which prevents any conformance to Christ through transformation of the passions.

The extreme positions highlighted above are foreign to Orthodoxy, the living experience of Christ evidenced throughout the ages by the astonishing variety of saints, men and women of every social class and ethnic background (Gal 3:28). This experience continues to be facilitated through personal effort, such as repetition of the Jesus Prayer and asceticism, as well as participation in the wider life of the church, especially the sacraments.

It is noteworthy that the New Testament has been composed in the Greek language, whose term for repentance is μετάνοια.[1] This noun stems from μετανοέω, which is comprised of a prefix denoting change and a verb signifying "I think," "I intend."[2] Rather than mere regret, repentance in the Greek Orthodox Church thus denotes a thorough transformation of one's

---

1. For a critical edition of the Greek text, see *Novum Testamentum Graece*, 28th ed. (complete details within the bibliography).

2. Liddell et al., *Greek-English Lexicon*, "μετά" and "νοέω," 1109, 1177.

perceptions and motivations, namely for the purpose of making oneself more receptive to Christ's salvific ministry and, in turn, worthy of his kingdom (Matt 3:2, 4:17; Mark 1:14–15).

The church teaches us that the major prerequisite for any spiritual change is humility, that we must first admit our limitations to God. Certainly, the meek fisherman, Simon, the son of Jonah, demonstrated this in one of his initial encounters with Christ (Matt 4:18–22; Mark 1:16–20; Luke 5:1–11). When he miraculously caught many fish at the Lord's command in a spot that he knew to be empty—having just labored there all night—Simon immediately confessed that he was a sinner. Profoundly aware of his own faults, the fisherman was terrified in the presence of Christ, to the extent that he even begged him to leave (Luke 5:8). Due to his meekness and honesty, however, the Lord recruited Simon as a "fisher of men" (ἁλιεὺς ἀνθρώπων). So began his lifelong dedication to the Lord, one which would make him not only a saint but a "Pillar of the Church."

Even in this early encounter with Christ we can detect a pattern that recurred throughout Simon's life, specifically humble acknowledgement of his sinful nature and a subsequent call to action. Granted, owing to his ardent faith, Simon was the first amongst the Disciples to recognize Jesus as God. This was shown at his saving confession, an event which marked the establishment of the church and which earned him the honorific "Cephas"/"Peter" (Matt 16:13–20; Mark 8:27–30; Luke 9:18–20). It was also demonstrated at the transfiguration, which he was deemed worthy to witness together with the "Sons of Thunder," Sts. James and John (Matt 17:1–8; Mark 9:2–8; Luke 9:28–36).

Yet there were also times when Simon became too confident in his own abilities whilst neglecting to trust in Providence, even though he had been exalted as Peter, the "Rock of Faith." For instance, he almost drowned whilst attempting to walk on water in imitation of Christ (Matt 14:22–33). He also attempted to discourage the Lord from facing his passion, as though he knew what was best for him (Matt 16:22; Mark 8:32). Moreover, he hastily proclaimed that he had the fortitude to stand by Christ during his suffering (Matt 26:31–35; Mark 14:27–31; Luke 22:31–34; John 13:36–38). As we know, Peter went on to repeatedly deny the Lord in the courtyard of the high priest, despite having been explicitly warned of this (Matt 26:57–58, 69–75; Mark 14:53–54, 66–72; Luke 22:54–62; John 18:15–18, 25–27). It should be noted that Peter's denial during Christ's trial was complete as suggested by the number of times that it was repeated (three signifies fulfilment in our tradition). Moreover, the apostle contradicted his saving confession by referring to Christ as a mere "man" (ἄνθρωπος), even cursing and rejecting any association with him (Mark 14:71).

Nevertheless, Peter immediately demonstrated his spiritual maturity through tears of compunction. In fact, he eventually displayed the bravery required of all Christians by running to the Lord's tomb upon hearing news of the resurrection (John 20:3–4, 6–7). Furthermore, following John's recognition of the Lord as he called out from the shore, Peter exhibited his consuming love for him by plunging into the waters without a second thought (John 21:7). It ought to be emphasized that these external actions were the result of an inner conversion, a change of awareness and intention on the part of the saint (i.e., repentance in the manner outlined above). Christ, following the resurrection, became the lens through which Peter viewed the world, his very reason for being.

The Lord soon recommissioned Peter as the leader of the disciples via a threefold confession of love, as recorded in John 21:15–19. It is often assumed that the Lord's three questions to Peter hurt him by reminding him of his denials, namely on the basis of John's affirmation that the apostle was "grieved" (ἐλυπήθη). Yet is it not more likely that Christ's restoration would have caused Peter to rejoice, whatever form it might have taken? Once again, we are obliged to turn our attention to the original Greek text. Here, we discover that Peter's heart was wounded because he perceived that he was not able to offer the self emptying and self-sacrificial love that the Lord had displayed towards him and all of humanity through his passion, as signified by the word ἀγάπη. More to the point, he recalled the Lord's declaration at the Mystical Supper that "Greater love (μείζονα ἀγάπην) has no one than this, than to lay down one's life for his friends (John 15:13 NKJV)." Indeed, in John 21 Christ uses the word ἀγαπάω the first two times that he asks Peter, "Do you love me?" He ultimately concedes to the simpler devotion that the apostle can offer using φιλέω; a verb which denotes the casual affection shown amongst friends (φίλοι).[3]

It is significant that the first and last letters of ἀγαπάω are the very same with which the Lord Jesus has identified himself as the beginning and end of all things (Rev 21:6). Since Christ is of the same essence as God the Father, and the Father is love (1 John 4:7–21), it follows that love is our eternal foundation and ultimate destiny. Love is essential for deification, a major means by which we may share in the life of the Holy Trinity. Christ

3. *Orthodox Study Bible*, 1467.

therefore remedied Peter's grief by reassuring him that he would become a "god by grace" in displaying his supreme love for the Trinity and the church through his eventual martyrdom (John 21:18–19).

Nevertheless, Peter fell at least once more according to tradition, that is, when he cut himself off from a large portion of the church in Antioch by refusing to eat with its gentile members. The apostle's motivation in this regard was to appease certain visitors from Jerusalem who maintained the old dietary laws (Gal 2:11–21). In other words, Peter prioritized the old Jewish law over the two commandments upon which it rested: i.e., love God with all your heart and your neighbor as yourself (Matt 22:35–40; Mark 12:28–34; Luke 10:25–28). This was despite the fact that he had been explicitly shown that the former dietary restrictions had been rendered obsolete through Christ's establishment of the New Covenant (Acts 10:9–16). As is well known, St. Paul of Tarsus publicly rebuked Peter for prioritizing what had become an ethnic custom above those of the church.

The incident at Antioch was the subject of some debate amongst Sts. Jerome of Stridon and Augustine of Hippo, two prominent theologians and interpreters of Scripture of the fourth century. In short, Jerome believed that Peter and Paul feigned a dispute in the city so that they might pacify and unite its Jewish and gentile Christians. The church father maintained that Peter condescended to the weaknesses of the visitors from Jerusalem to avoid offending them and thus keep them from separating themselves from the faith community. Peter therefore offered his co-worker Paul the opportunity to remedy his Jewish followers' divisive attitude through his own chastisement, reconciling them to their offended, former pagan, siblings.[4]

Whilst respectfully challenging Jerome's interpretation, Augustine insisted that Peter was genuinely afraid of offending the visitors and subsequently mistaken in attempting to impose on others an ethnic custom that he was merely pretending to observe. He nonetheless extolled the apostle for his humility in publicly accepting correction, asserting that he proved to be the "more admirable and difficult to imitate" in allowing himself to be admonished by a junior for the benefit of the church.[5] For Augustine, it was a matter of defending the authenticity of the Scriptures, which he argued should not be interpreted as justifying any acts of deceit lest the authority

4. Jerome of Stridon, *Commentary on Galatians*, 105–10.

5. Augustine of Hippo, *Commentary on Galatians* 15.7–10, 144–45.

of its doctrinal and practical exhortations be questioned.[6] He eventually convinced Jerome of his position.[7]

Moving on to another possible instance in which the apostle fell, in the apocryphal *Acts of Peter* we read that he initially attempted to flee his martyrdom. The *Acts* relate that Peter had in fact escaped execution in Rome under the pretext of preaching elsewhere when he suddenly met the Lord walking towards the city. According to the anonymous author, Christ told Peter that he was going to be crucified again, thus bringing him to his senses and compelling him to bear the ultimate witness to the gospel. Having gladly returned to the city to be executed, Peter demonstrated his characteristic virtue of humility by requesting to be crucified upside down in a manner evocative of his fallen nature rather than the Lord's divinity.[8]

Whatever the authenticity of the Acts, we may be confident that Peter demonstrated throughout his life that humility is a major requirement for genuine repentance. The apostle accepted correction from both his master, Christ, and his junior, Paul. He never attempted to hide his faults, allowing even his greatest moments of weakness to be related to the church, to every generation of the faithful. We may ask why the "Pillar" of the church was permitted to fall in the first place. St. Gregory the Great, a celebrated hagiographer and the bishop responsible for the first mission to the Anglo-Saxons, has provided us with a moving answer. In his *Homilies on the Gospels*, the church father affirms that Peter was permitted to fail owing to his vocation as a chief shepherd, so that he might have compassion on his flock: "that he might perceive from his own weakness how mercifully he ought to put up with the weaknesses of others."[9] This interpretation no doubt serves as a consolation for us, teaching us that our greatest spiritual challenges are intended to engender sympathy for our weaker brothers and sisters in Christ.

At this point, it is worth evaluating Peter's legacy as a penitent as tacitly reflected in the sayings of the desert fathers and mothers. We see that the apostle never gave in to despair and listlessness, even when he denied the Lord. This is in stark contrast to Judas, who did not attempt to repent in the appropriate manner and therefore took his own life (Matt

---

6. Augustine of Hippo, *Select Letters*, 60–67.

7. For evidence that Jerome finally shared Augustine's perception of the incident at Antioch, see: Jerome of Stridon, *Against the Pelagians* 1.22, 460.

8. *Acts of Peter*, 35–39, 114–20.

9. Gregory the Great, *Forty Gospel Homilies* 21, 160.

27:3–10). These figures thus typify the two forms of grief defined by St. Syncletica of Alexandria. According to Syncletica, the first, positive form stems from the recognition of one's own weaknesses and those of their fellow Christians for the purpose of reminding oneself of life's true purpose and attaching oneself to God. The church mother emphasized that the other, destructive form "comes from the enemy, full of mockery" and "must be cast out, mainly by prayer and psalmody."[10]

What is more, we are called to recognize from Peter's life that we will likely fall countless times on our journey to the kingdom, notwithstanding our respective charisms. However, we must always attempt to get back up, remembering that we have the power to renew ourselves at any given moment by God's grace. When asked by St. Moses the Ethiopian whether it is possible for a believer to lay a new spiritual foundation every day, St. Silvanus of Scetis affirmed that "If he works hard, he can lay a new foundation at every moment."[11] To be sure, when asked by a brother who was struggling to redeem himself how many times he should continue to rise, St. Sisoes the Great responded: "Until you are taken up either in virtue or in sin. For a man presents himself to judgement in the state in which he is found."[12] Elder Thaddeus of Vitovnica, a renowned spiritual guide of Serbia during the twentieth century, wonderfully reiterated Sisoes' instruction, adding that "Even if we fall a hundred times a day it does not matter; we must get up and go on walking toward God without looking back."[13]

Undoubtedly, Peter serves as one of our most important models of repentance. We are incredibly blessed to comprise his greatest legacy, the Orthodox Church. The church is truly the body of Christ, providing us with the best means of mending ourselves: e.g., the sacraments of confession, holy unction, and the Eucharist. Her holy mysteries enable the genuine imitation of Peter, including his personal repentance. Moreover, the church makes it possible for us to celebrate and directly communicate with the beloved chief of the apostles and similar paragons through the beautiful hymns of her liturgical services. May we all attain Peter's faith, humility, and perfect love for the Lord that we may contribute to the life of the church in a manner which makes him proud.

10. *Sayings of the Desert Fathers*, 235.
11. *Sayings of the Desert Fathers*, 224.
12. *Sayings of the Desert Fathers*, 220.
13. *Our Thoughts Determine Our Lives*, 104.

2

Christian Identity as Articulated by St. Paul and the Early Church Fathers

But after faith has come, we are no longer under a tutor. For you are all sons of God through faith in Christ Jesus. For as many of you as were baptized into Christ have put on Christ. There is neither Jew nor Greek, there is neither slave nor free, there is neither male nor female; for you are all one in Christ Jesus. And if you are Christ's, then you are Abraham's seed, and heirs according to the promise.[1]—St. Paul the Apostle (Gal 3:26–29 NKJV)

THE CONVICTION THAT ONE'S identity in Christ should take precedence over their ethnicity, social status, and gender is rooted within the Apostolic tradition which constitutes the bedrock of Orthodoxy. St. Paul the Apostle intimated that, for those who comprise the church, faith in the Lord and its resulting moral lifestyle ought to be valued above every other qualification, whether cultural, communal, or biological. To this end, his authoritative understanding of a church which eclipses—yet neither disparages or abolishes—societal distinctions is expounded upon by Sts. John Chrysostom, Jerome of Stridon, and Augustine of Hippo in their respective commentaries on Galatians.

Paul wrote his letter to the Galatians in the mid-first century to correct his followers' understanding of the gospel after it had been corrupted

---

1. Gal 3:26 mirrors Gal 3:28–29. See Heidebrecht, "Distinction and Function in the Church," 183.

by a group of schismatics commonly referred to as "Judaizers."[2] After embracing the gospel as it was received by the apostle in its entirety through a direct encounter with the glorified Christ (Gal 1:1, 11–12), the Galatians had turned to unorthodox teachings which claimed that all Christians must observe the precepts of the Jewish law to be saved, particularly the right of circumcision.[3] In response—and in contrast to the antique Jewish teachings which prevented gentiles, slaves, and women from participating in the religious life—Paul reiterated that justification by faith had been prioritized over observance of the law during Abraham's time, when the eventual conversion of the gentiles had been foreseen (Gal 3:6–9).[4] He therefore asserted that one's identity in Christ can only be guaranteed by the former together with the sacrament of baptism. In other words, the saint argued that the nomistic observances established to safeguard the people of God and prepare them for the coming of the Messiah had been abolished through our Lord's saving passion so that men and women of all nations might constitute one spiritual family.

John Chrysostom wrote his *Commentary on Galatians* when he was bishop of Antioch sometime after 395. The text is unique since Chrysostom has not concluded the homilies which comprise it with moral or practical exhortations according to his custom. The commentary is still didactic, featuring reprovals against all manner of heresies that might result from doctrinal error, especially Marcionism and Manichaeism.[5]

2. Just Jr., "Apostolic Councils of Galatians and Acts," 279; Hopko, "Galatians 3:28," 173.

3. For more on the direct revelation of the gospel experienced by Paul, see: John Chrysostom, *Commentary on the Epistle to the Galatians*," 19; Jerome of Stridon, *Commentary on Galatians*, 80–81. The schismatics who disturbed the mainstream Christian communities located in Galatia were like those that the apostle had been required to oppose at Antioch and caused his dispute with St. Peter. Just Jr, "Apostolic Councils of Galatians and Acts," 275.

4. Uzukwu, "Gal 3,28 and Its Alleged Relationship to Rabbinic Writings," 379–80; Hopko, "Galatians 3:28," 176.

5. In short, Marcion and his followers accepted certain parts of the New Testament but denied our Lord's humanity whilst condemning the representation of God in the Old Testament. Meanwhile, Mani and his supporters attempted to amalgamate different faiths whilst condemning matter and promoting themselves as the custodians of special "truths." For evidence of the church father's refutation of Manichaeism and Marcionism, see: John Chrysostom, *Commentary on the Epistle to the Galatians*, 9, 13–14, 79.

Jerome composed his analysis of the Pauline letter in 386, dedicating it to his patrons Marcella, Paula, and Eustochium.[6] Despite being composed in haste, the text consists of three comprehensive books, with Jerome drawing upon a range of classical and Eastern patristic sources.[7] Much like Chrysostom, Jerome has used his interpretation as a means of censuring numerous heresies, including Marcionism.[8]

Augustine wrote his *Commentary on Galatians* between 394 and 395.[9] Augustine's commentary resembles those of Chrysostom and Jerome, featuring overt and implicit refutations of multiple heresies (e.g., Manichaeism, Donatism, and Arianism).[10] Interestingly, Augustine has also criticized certain pagan practices that were still common amongst Christians during his time within the text.[11]

In the passage cited at the beginning of this chapter, Paul refers to the law as a disciplinarian—a tutor intended to prepare the people of God for the coming of their Savior—implying that the Old and New Covenants are in accord.[12] The apostle conveys his belief in the continuity between the Christian and Jewish traditions earlier within the same chapter, basing it on the doctrine of justification by faith: "just as Abraham 'believed God, and it was accounted to him for righteousness.' Therefore know that only those who are of faith are sons of Abraham (Gal 3:6–7 NKJV)."

Chrysostom affirms in his commentary that the apostle mentioned Abraham's faith to refute those who had made the Galatians afraid to abandon the Jewish cultural customs they felt had bound them to the Old Testament figure.[13] Interpreting Gal 3:6, John indicates that the apostle went a

---

6. Cain, "Introduction" to Jerome of Stridon, *Commentary on Galatians*, 16–17.

7. Cain, "Introduction" to Jerome of Stridon, *Commentary on Galatians*, 19–30.

8. Cain, "Introduction" to Jerome of Stridon, *Commentary on Galatians*, 41–49.

9. Plumer, "Introduction" to Augustine of Hippo, *Augustine's Commentary on Galatians*, 3, 6.

10. Plumer, "Introduction" to Augustine of Hippo, *Augustine's Commentary on Galatians*, 61–71.

11. The Donatists had separated themselves from the wider church owing to their radical austerity and obstinate refusal to forgive Christians who had surrendered to the Roman state during the Great Persecution that took place under the pagan emperor Diocletian. Plumer, "Introduction" to Augustine of Hippo, *Augustine's Commentary on Galatians*, 68–70.

12. See also: John Chrysostom, *Commentary on the Epistle to the Galatians*, 59–60; Jerome of Stridon, *Commentary on Galatians*, 150–51.

13. John Chrysostom, *Commentary on the Epistle to the Galatians*, 52.

step further in suggesting that members of the church are more privileged than the patriarch since the law has since been fulfilled by Christ and superseded by the gospel.[14] Nevertheless, the importance that the apostle placed on the association between Abraham and the Incarnate Lord in Gal 3:16 is not challenged by the church father.[15] On the contrary, the saint interprets Gal 3:26–27 as pertaining to the bond shared between Abraham, Christ, and all adherents of the New Covenant.[16] The church father considers Christians to be sons of Abraham in their imitation of his confidence and commitment to God. However, they are also sons of God for having faith comparable to that of the patriarch and taken on the moral and spiritual responsibilities which baptism entails. Chrysostom was convinced that the apostle had appropriately demonstrated that faith was anterior to the law and intended for the justification of the gentiles, so that the patriarch rejoiced in anticipation of their conversion.[17]

Interestingly, Jerome has expressed a similar conviction. Although the church father claimed that the relationship between Abraham and the Incarnate Lord is more direct on the basis of genealogy, he nonetheless asserted that those who believe in the Son of God are the progeny of both in light of their devotion to the same gospel.[18] Chrysostom and Jerome likewise maintained that Paul viewed the church as a family consisting of Jews and gentiles united in faith and no longer bound or divided by cultural precepts.

Chrysostom reiterated that both Jews and gentiles have become mysteriously united with the Savior through the sacrament of baptism: "If Christ be the Son of God, and thou hast put on Him, thou who hast the Son within thee, and art fashioned after His pattern, hast been brought into one kindred and nature with Him."[19] The Incarnate Lord is seen by John as both

14. "And if he who was before grace, was justified by Faith, although plentiful in works, much more shall ye." John Chrysostom, *Commentary on the Epistle to the Galatians*, 52.

15. "Now to Abraham and his Seed were the promises made. He does not say, 'And to seeds,' as of many, but as of one, 'And to your Seed,' who is Christ" (Gal 3:16 NKJV).

16. John Chrysostom, *Commentary on the Epistle to the Galatians*, 52–53, 60.

17. John Chrysostom, *Commentary on the Epistle to the Galatians*, 53.

18. Jerome of Stridon, *Commentary on Galatians*, 152–53.

19. John Chrysostom, *Commentary on the Epistle to the Galatians*, 60. This was also considered by Augustine. Relating Gal 3:16 and 28 to Col 1:18, he affirmed that Paul "shows that the one seed [of Abraham], Christ, signifies not only the Mediator himself but also the Church, of which he is the head of the body." Augustine of Hippo, *Augustine's*

the archetype (i.e., the model) and the *telos* (i.e., the ultimate object or aim) of humanity. According to Chrysostom, it follows that those who have formally embraced the Christian faith have risen above the many cultural and social divisions that once separated them from their maker and each other, arriving at a state of holiness: "He that was a Greek, or Jew, or bond-man yesterday, carries about with him the form, not of an Angel or Archangel, but of the Lord of all, yea displays in his own person the Christ."[20] The church father thus hints at the doctrine of deification while interpreting the revolutionary passage from Galatians, much like Jerome, who claimed that

> [w]hen someone definitely clothes himself with Christ and is cast into the flame and glimmers with the intense brightness of the Holy Spirit, it is impossible to tell whether he is gold or silver. As long as the lump of the material is surrounded by the heat, it has a uniform fiery color, and all diversity of its nature, condition, and physical properties is taken away by this cloak.[21]

Jerome's striking image of the baptized Christian alludes to the Lord's splendid appearance on Mount Tabor (Matt 17:1–8; Mark 9:2–8; Luke 9:28–36; and 2 Pet 1:16–18), on the one hand, and the desert fathers' experience of God's uncreated energies in the form of divine light, on the other. It is noteworthy that he has offered this image while explaining the distinction between whom he perceives to be true and false Christians. Indeed, the church father maintained that the sacrament of baptism is not enough to transform one into a genuine Christian. It is also a matter of "clothing" oneself with Christ by embracing the gift of the Holy Spirit, confessing the appropriate doctrines, and engaging in Orthopraxis:

> If anyone has received only the bodily baptism of water that is visible to fleshly eyes, he has not clothed himself with the Lord Jesus Christ. For Simon [the magician] in the Acts of the Apostles had received the baptism of water, yet he had not clothed himself with Christ because he did not have the Holy Spirit. Furthermore, the heretics, hypocrites, and those who lead morally reprehensible lives appear on the surface to receive baptism, but I do not know if they have the clothing of Christ.[22]

Commentary on Galatians 28.6, 175.

20. John Chrysostom, *Commentary on the Epistle to the Galatians*, 61.

21. Jerome of Stridon, *Commentary on Galatians*, 152.

22. Jerome of Stridon, *Commentary on Galatians*, 151–52.

At this point, it must be emphasized that Paul did not suggest that humanity's cultural, social, and gender-related distinctions are erased through baptism.[23] Chrysostom, Jerome, and Augustine shed some light on this matter, highlighting that the many adherents of the church—individual sovereigns simultaneously buttressed and undermined by their cultural contexts—are distinct from the world by their saving confession which in turns guides their moral conduct. The church is egalitarian insofar as it is open to all. However, it is ultimately represented by those who truly aspire to imitate Christ, whatever their inevitable failings. According to Augustine, the church consists of a limited portion of the entire global population, albeit one drawn from all nations:

> These people, if considered throughout the whole world—for he [i.e., God] gathers the Church, the heavenly Jerusalem, from the whole world—are still few, because the narrow way is found by few. Yet as many as have been able to come forth since the proclamation of the gospel, and as many as are able to come forth throughout all nations until the end of the world, are gathered into one. These people, together with those, though very few, who obtained the salvation of grace by faith in the Lord (that is, prophetic faith before both of his comings) fill the most blessed state of the saints of the eternal city.[24]

The patristic commentators teach us that Paul contributed to the social cohesion of the early church by promoting ontological equality. Augustine went a step further in exploring the sociological implications of the apostle's letter, affirming that—even though the flock can mystically experience oneness in Christ as a foretaste through baptism and the sacramental life more generally—certain ethnic, social, and gender-related distinctions will persist in this age:

> For now, although we have the first-fruits of the spirit (Rom 8:23), which is life, on account of the righteousness of faith, yet because the body is still dead on account of sin, that difference, whether of peoples or of legal status or of sex, while indeed already removed in the unity of faith, remains in the mortal life [. . .]. For there are some things which we observe in the unity of the faith without any distinction, and other things which we observe in the order

---

23. Hopko, "Galatians 3:28," 173, 180–81.

24. Augustine of Hippo, *Augustine's Commentary on Galatians* 24.13, 167.

> of this life as on a journey, lest the name and teaching of God be blasphemed (1 Tim 6:1).[25]

Augustine subsequently maintained that the present life is transient in nature, that Christians are sojourners who conform to the world's fleeting social conventions while maintaining their spiritual integrity. The church father held that social differences, whatever their time and place, are unavoidable so long as we remain subject to the cosmological consequences of sin. Furthermore, he posited that that the disruption of certain conventions might adversely impact the welfare of the church (perhaps, one may speculate, by scandalizing potential converts). His stance echoes the Lord's call for us to observe our prevailing civil requirements which do not contradict his gospel (Matt 22:15–22; Mark 12:13–17; Luke 20:20–26). Augustine also stated that our ethnic and social qualifications will finally be eclipsed in the age to come.[26]

It is evident that the patristic commentaries examined above remain true to the teachings of St. Paul, demanding earnest faith in Christ from all believers. Sts. John Chrysostom, Jerome, and Augustine similarly related Galatians to their immediate circumstances to defend the doctrinal integrity of the church. They also articulated a variety of identity-markers that have endured for centuries within the Christian tradition. More precisely, Chrysostom and Jerome maintained that the ethnic, social, and gendered characteristics which divide us can be transcended in the here and now by those who experience deification. While Chrysostom suggested that believers of the New Covenant constitute a spiritual family together with Abraham—united in Christ through baptism and by sharing in the patriarch's faith—Jerome differentiated between genuine and faux Christians. To be more exact, the latter highlighted that the identity-altering sacrament of baptism is realized through the confession of the correct dogma and a lifestyle consistent with that of Christ and his saints. Meanwhile, Augustine explicitly related Galatians to the social interactions of the faithful, suggesting that Christians must observe certain worldly distinctions until they are fully eclipsed in the next life. In the final analysis, Paul's letter

---

25. Augustine of Hippo, *Augustine's Commentary on Galatians* 28.3–4, 173–75.

26. "In this faith there is no distinction between Jew and Greek, slave and free, male and female; since all have been baptized, all are one in Christ Jesus. And if this is accomplished by faith, by which we walk righteously in this life, how much more perfectly and completely will it be accomplished by sight itself, when we see face to face (1 Cor 3:12)?" Augustine of Hippo, *Augustine's Commentary on Galatians* 28.1–2, 173.

inspired the church fathers to positively articulate a Christian identity which rises above nationalist exclusivism, shallow ritualism, and immoral ideologies that disrupt social cohesion.

3

Martyrdom, the Eucharist, and the Courage of the Saints

> It is to Him, as the Son of God, that we give our adoration; while to the martyrs, as disciples and imitators of the Lord, we give the love they have earned by their matchless devotion to their King and Teacher. Pray God we too may come to share their company and their discipleship.—*The Martyrdom of Polycarp* 17 (second century AD)[1]

THE INITIAL PERSECUTION OF our Christian forebears was partly a result of their expulsion from the Jewish synagogues, which had been declared beforehand by our Lord and Savior (John 16:1–4).[2] Consequently, the church was excluded from the religious traditions permitted by Roman law, which also encompassed numerous pagan cults and philosophical schools. In fact, the faithful were originally perceived by the wider world as constituting a treacherous sect; a view which gained currency through a variety of slanders on the part of both pagans and Jews. The situation was further aggravated by the various gnostic factions; exclusivists who appropriated aspects of Christianity within eccentric and absurd belief systems, and with whom the fathers had to contend for centuries.

---

1. I am indebted to my brother, Dr. Mario Baghos, for his useful insights concerning the phenomenon of martyrdom and the account of Polycarp's passion. *Martyrdom of Polycarp* 17, 131.

2. Kesich, *Formation and Struggles*, 139.

The mad emperor, Nero, was among the first and worst opponents of the early church, having used it as a scapegoat for a certain fire in Rome which he probably started himself. The church thus did not acquire a crucial privilege that had been granted to the Jewish people, namely, exemption from participating in the ruler cult. The living emperors of Rome after the reign of Augustus were actually worshipped as gods, and it became widely accepted that their veneration through oaths and offerings of incense and slaughtered animals ensured the peace of the inhabited world.[3] The faithful were clearly faced with a major problem: to participate in the pagan ritual practices contradicted the church's fundamental tenets (Exod 20:1–6; Deut 5:6–10), yet failure to do so would result in ruthless persecution by the state.

While the cruel treatment of the church was sporadic in the Roman world until the accession of St. Constantine the Great, countless followers of the Son and Word of God—Greeks and Jews, slaves and freedmen, men and women—were unjustly executed over the first four centuries. This led to numerous eyewitness accounts of major instances of martyrdom that took place throughout the Greek East and Latin West, especially during the reigns of Antoninus Pius, Marcus Aurelius, and Diocletian. Many of these records have managed to survive—albeit with varying degrees of literary embellishment for the purpose of catechetical instruction and conversion—disclosing the relationship between the early church and the pagan empire.

The leaders of Rome were initially uncertain how to respond to Christianity, which they understood as a "new" religion, having had no interest in the fulfilment of the Jewish prophecies. Pliny the Younger, a legate to Pontus-Bithynia on the southern shore of the Black Sea, therefore decided to contact his emperor, Trajan, via letter to determine how to best manage those who refused to attend pagan temples and purchase sacrificed meat. In refusing to perform these tasks, the faithful were also seen to be deliberately undermining the economy of the empire.[4] In his letter, Pliny described the procedure which he used to identify and condemn Christ's followers:

> I asked them whether they were Christians. If they admitted it,
> I asked a second and a third time, threatening them with execu-
> tion. Those who remained obdurate I ordered to be executed, for
> I was in no doubt, whatever it was which they were confessing,

---

3. Kesich, *Formation and Struggles*, 139.

4. Kesich, *Formation and Struggles*, 141.

> that their obstinacy and their inflexible stubbornness should at
> any rate be punished.[5]

Trajan directly replied that Pliny was to punish those who were reported but pardon anyone who denied their faith by offering prayers to the pagan gods, in this manner defining the empire's custom regarding the treatment of fervent Christians.[6] Yet the reasons behind the alleged "obstinacy" of the Orthodox can be inferred from the books of the New Testament, which were compiled in this period. For the church, Christ remained "the faithful witness, the firstborn from the dead, and the ruler over the kings of the earth" (Rev 1:5 NKJV). It was inconceivable for the saints to denounce the Lord in favor of an idol, hence the refusal on the part of many to purchase and eat meat sacrificed to the emperor and other pagan deities (which abstinence was ultimately promoted by St. Paul for the sake of compassion and unity, 1 Cor 8:4–13). Instead, they openly confessed Christ, knowing that they would be declared righteous by him in the presence of the angels (Luke 12:8–9).

It is necessary to emphasize that the martyrs were not motivated by fear of eternal punishment, but by their perfect love for Christ. St. Polycarp, the second-century bishop of Smyrna and direct disciple of St. John the Evangelist, is a notable example in this regard. Polycarp was one of the many martyrs sentenced to be consumed by fire in public display. His execution was committed in the arena of his city, in which he was brought for trial by the proconsul (i.e., governor) of the wider region. The official insisted that the church father deny Christ, adhering to a method like that stipulated by Trajan. Despite the proconsul's threats of wild beasts and flames, Polycarp refused to deny the Lord.[7] His motivation is wonderfully reflected in the following assertion that he made while on trial: "Eighty and six years have I served [Christ], and He has done me no wrong. How then can I blaspheme my King and my Saviour?"[8] Other forms of punishment that were practiced against the faithful at the time included beheading, crucifixion, and being thrown to wild animals for mauling and live consumption. Those who were captured had the reassurance of the Holy Spirit, knowing that they would act accordingly when brought before the authorities. Certainly, they knew

---

5. Pliny the Younger, *Complete Letters* 10.96.3–4, 278.

6. Pliny the Younger, *Complete Letters* 10.97.1–2, 279.

7. *Martyrdom of Polycarp* 9–10, 128–29.

8. *Martyrdom of Polycarp* 9, 128.

that Christ himself had foretold their circumstances when he had sent out his apostles (Matt 10:17–20).

The gospels were undoubtedly a major influence on the church's understanding of martyrdom, especially the accounts of Christ's saving passion. Parallels between the capture and sentence of a believer, on the one hand, and the Lord's betrayal, trial, and crucifixion, on the other, were taken as signs of Divine Providence. Serenity and humility were among the most important similarities. Members of the church were thus discouraged from actively seeking out the authorities to attain a heroic death. This is evidenced by the account of Quintus the Phrygian in the *Martyrdom of Polycarp* 4. In short, Quintus surrendered himself to the authorities when Polycarp was being sought for arrest. His zeal was such that he managed to compel others to follow him yet, in the end, his "courage failed him at the sight of the beasts" which were to carry out his execution. And so, at the behest of the proconsul, Quintus took the customary oath to the emperor, also offering the required incense before his image.[9]

Polycarp "showed not the least sign of alarm" at the news of the warrant for his capture. Yet he was convinced by his friends to withdraw from his city and take refuge at a nearby farm. Displaying no fear at the prospect of being tried and slayed, he used the situation to ceaselessly pray "for churches all over the world, as it was his usual habit to do."[10] Yet the author of the martyr act relates that Polycarp attempted to escape the authorities once more.[11] This does not imply that he was afraid of death but seeking to adhere to the Lord's exhortation: "When they persecute you in this city, flee to another" (Matt 10:23 NKJV). In other words, the saint was attempting to carry out his apostolic work for as long as was possible despite his advanced age. Polycarp eventually resigned to the authorities in a manner reminiscent of our Lord's submission. Like Christ, the saint was betrayed by his own (Matt 26:14–16; Mark 14:10–11; Luke 23:3–5).

Polycarp's older friend, St. Ignatius of Antioch, likewise displayed the compassion and altruism characteristic of the early martyrs.[12] On the

9. *Martyrdom of Polycarp* 4, 126.

10. *Martyrdom of Polycarp* 5, 126.

11. *Martyrdom of Polycarp* 6, 126–27.

12. Ignatius was a fellow disciple of John according to tradition and his letter of counsel to Polycarp is full of affection. Polycarp's reverence for Ignatius is evidenced by his hortatory epistle to the Philippian Christian community, in which he refers to his friend as a paragon of the faith, informing them that he will forward all the correspondence which he has received from him in accordance with their request. See: Ignatius of

way to his trial and execution in Rome, where he was fed to lions, Ignatius prioritized his responsibility of maintaining harmony throughout the church. For instance, he wrote a letter to the flock in Smyrna informing them that peace had been restored to the church in Antioch. He therefore exhorted the Smyrnaeans to send someone to congratulate their Antiochian brothers and sisters, to bolster affection between the two communities.[13] More importantly, the church father emphasized the certainty of Christ's bodily passion and resurrection to fortify them against the heretics plaguing their city; the Docetists, who falsely taught the Lord was an incorporeal spirit which only seemed to be human.[14] The saint therefore comforted the faithful in Smyrna while stressing the reality of the incarnation, insisting that his ability to endure persecution for the sake of the gospel was inspired by the genuine physical trials experienced by Christ who had risen and was empowering him.[15]

Sadly, there are many intellectuals who argue that there was some justification for the cruelty displayed towards the early church since it refused to adhere to formal edicts. The reality is that the faithful were erroneously perceived as threats to the stability of what had until that time been a worldly kingdom largely characterized by superstition (the philosophical schools constituting a notable exception). The church ultimately favored obedience to God who was revealed in the person of Jesus Christ, not the emperor. In this respect, martyrs such as Polycarp and Ignatius did not go out of their way to defy the authorities or provoke their own deaths any more than the Lord himself had. At any rate, it is not a matter of whether the martyrs "deserved" to die. Rather, it is a matter of evaluating why they were and continue to be celebrated by the Orthodox.

The martyrs throughout the ages have imitated Christ and his apostles, who resisted all manner of dissuasion when confronted by the authorities. This has been made even more evident by their physical sacrifices. As a matter of fact, their deaths have benefited the entire world by rendering them mediators to God in aid of all creation. Interestingly, the church's worldwide adoration for the saints was anticipated by the (largely unknown) authors of the *Martyrdom of Polycarp*, Marcion and Evarestus,

---

Antioch, *Epistle to Polycarp* 1–8 (esp. 1–3 and 7–8), 109–12; Polycarp of Smyrna, *Epistle of Polycarp to the Philippians* 9 and 13, 122, 124.

13. Ignatius of Antioch, *Epistle to the Smyrnaeans* 11, 103–4.

14. Ignatius of Antioch, *Epistle to the Smyrnaeans* 1–7, 101–3.

15. Ignatius of Antioch, *Epistle to the Smyrnaeans* 4, 101–2.

who stated that the faithful vied to touch their subject's body and garments owing to his angelic life. Furthermore, the authors emphasized that Polycarp became like baking bread producing the aroma of incense while at the stake, that he was shown to be a very image of the Eucharist.[16]

Truly, the *Martyrdom of Polycarp* reveals that adversity, contempt, and even death were approached and patiently experienced by our forebears. The same can be inferred from Ignatius's *Letter to the Romans* 4. Here, the church father has presented martyrdom as a sacrament using the language of Holy Communion, suggesting that it similarly ensures direct participation in the Lord's passion and resurrection.[17] The saints understood that the genuine body and blood of the Lord offered during the Divine Liturgy obliged them to imitate his immense love for humankind, best demonstrated by his sufferings.

To be sure, St. Cyprian of Carthage, a martyr and renowned theologian of the third century, affirmed in a letter to the faithful in Thibaris (modern-day Thibar, Tunisia) that Holy Communion would prepare them for looming persecution, enabling them to endure it "with an incorrupt faith and robust courage" as "soldiers of Christ . . ."[18] A righteous death— voluntarily accepted, not presumptuously sought out—in the name of the Lord and for the sake of the gospel may therefore be considered the most authentic realization of the Eucharist, first offered to humankind on the eve of the passion (Matt 26:26–30; Mark 14:22–26; Luke 22:15–20). Cyprian eventually met such a glorious end during the savage persecution instigated by Valerian, bravely exclaiming "Thanks be to God!" (*Deo gratias*) when sentenced to be beheaded in public at Carthage by the proconsul, Galerius Maximus, on the 14th of September, 258.[19]

Martyrdom and the Eucharist are undeniably associated as expressions of thanksgiving. Ignatius thus described his life as a libation being poured upon an altar, pointing to Christ as his sole desire and expressing his disdain for worldly things.[20] Similarly, Polycarp has been depicted as both a sacrificial

16. *Martyrdom of Polycarp* 13–15, 129–30.

17. Ignatius of Antioch, *Epistle to the Romans* 4, 86; Johanny, "Ignatius of Antioch," 63–64; Clancy, "Imitating the Mysteries That You Celebrate," 110–13.

18. Cyprian of Carthage, *Letters 1–81*, 163; Clancy, "Imitating the Mysteries That You Celebrate," 123.

19. *Acts of St. Cyprian* 4, 172–73.

20. Ignatius of Antioch, *Epistle to the Romans* 2, 85–86; Clancy, "Imitating the Mysteries That You Celebrate," 110.

ram and a whole burnt offering by Marcion and Evarestus.[21] In fact, the authors have presented the church father as progressing through the pattern of the *anaphora*—the central aspect of the Liturgy, consisting in thanksgiving, petition, and doxology—during his final prayer in the flesh.[22]

Ignatius, Polycarp, and Cyprian subsequently challenge us to establish consistency between our participation in the Liturgy and our daily lives, having emphasized that earnest participation in the sacraments will lead to true love for the Lord that extends to the wider community—a love which knows no compromise. Through their words and deeds, the hierarchs and martyrs have shown us that the church's holy mysteries transform all who partake of them with ardent faith into "little Christs." Perhaps most significantly, they continue to remind us that we have nothing to fear in this world despite its inevitable physical and spiritual sufferings, which may result from a wide range of factors: e.g., religious discrimination, tyranny of the state, and even ignorance on the part of our dearest ones. Indeed, what cause have we to be afraid if even death—the worst possible outcome for our struggles in this world—has been utterly defeated by our Lord and Savior?

21. *Martyrdom of Polycarp* 14–15, 129–30; Clancy, "Imitating the Mysteries That You Celebrate," 114–15.

22. *Martyrdom of Polycarp* 14, 129–30; Clancy, "Imitating the Mysteries That You Celebrate," 114–17.

4

St. Justin, the Martyr and Philosopher

On the 1st of June, we commemorate our father among the saints, Justin, the martyr and philosopher. As his honorific titles suggest, Justin's defense of Orthodoxy was as fearless as it was brilliant. Drawing on his literary-rhetorical and philosophical training, this saint of tremendous importance gave his life in systematically refuting insults and rumors against the church on the part of both pagans and Jews, callous assertions that were causing numerous atrocities against the faithful. Subsequently, he was instrumental in defining the medieval Christian attitude towards classical culture.

Justin was born in Flavia Neapolis, Palestine (modern-day Nablus), during the late-first or early-second century and very likely descended from Greco-Roman colonists, judging from the names of his father and grandfather (Priscus and Bacchius, respectively). The church father probably proceeded through the classical education system typical of Late Antiquity, which consisted in the analysis and memorization of major poetical, historical, and oratorical works, including the literary figures and tropes featured therein.[1] He was certainly a seeker of wisdom prior to his adoption of Christianity, having earnestly attempted to become a Stoic, a Peripatetic, a Pythagorean, and a Platonist. Interestingly, Justin revealed that only his

1. Justin Martyr, Ἰουστίνου ἀπολογία ὑπὲρ Χριστιανῶν πρὸς Ἀντωνίνον τὸν Εὐσεβῆ [i.e., *First Apology*] 1.1, 80–81; Falls, "Foreword" to Justin Martyr, *First Apology*, 9; Minns and Parvis, "Introduction" to *Justin, Philosopher and Martyr*, 32; Barnard, *Justin Martyr*, 5; Penella, "Progymnasmata in Imperial Greek Education," 77; Kelly, *Golden Mouth*, 6; Baur, *Antioch*, 10–11; Lee, "Why Didn't St Basil Write in New Testament Greek?" 10.

Platonist teacher offered him any knowledge of God and intelligible realities, the Stoic having considered such information unnecessary, the Peripatetic having been more concerned with payment, and the Pythagorean having demanded that he first learn music, astronomy, and geometry.[2]

Justin's conversion to Christianity occurred when he met a mysterious sage during one of his habitual meditative walks near the sea. In short, the mystic convinced Justin that he had fallen into grave contradictions with respect to his understanding of the human soul and its relation to God. When Justin realized that his cherished Platonists had failed to apprehend such realities, he asked the old man which teacher or method he ought to follow. The sage directed him to the Old Testament prophets, specifically their noble manner of life, their writings, and their miracles, how they exalted God the Father through such means and, just as importantly, made the Son known to humankind.[3]

Andrew Hofer convincingly argued that the church father implied in his account of this event that the old mystic was, in fact, our Lord and Savior Jesus Christ, albeit mystically concealed. This is because there are at least fifteen parallels between Justin's description of his encounter with the mysterious figure and that of Cleopas and his companion with the God-man on the road to Emmaus (Luke 24:13–35). These include (amongst other things) initial feigned ignorance on the part of the teacher intended to expose the false thinking of their listener(s); the former's mysterious appearance and vanishing; and an interpretation of the Old Testament leading to illumination, warmth in the heart, and a desire to proclaim the gospel. Moreover, the mystic can be taken as the "Ancient of Days" referred to in the Scriptures, traditionally identified as the Lord Jesus by the church (Dan 7:9–10, 13–14, 22; Rev 1).[4]

Having encountered Christ face to face, Justin immediately devoted the remainder of his life to the defense and dissemination of the gospel. This is evidenced by his surviving works, particularly his first and second *Apologies*. These texts are not admissions of error or guilt as the term "apology" typically suggests today. They are instead sophisticated justifications of the Christian faith and rituals for which countless were being persecuted throughout Late Antiquity, especially during the reign of Marcus Aurelius.[5]

---

2. Justin Martyr, *Dialogue with Trypho* 2.3–6, 5–7.

3. Justin Martyr, *Dialogue with Trypho* 3–8.2, 7–15.

4. Hofer, "Old Man as Christ in Justin's 'Dialogue with Trypho,'" 1–21.

5. Baghos, "Apologetic and Literary Value of the *Acts of Justin*," 46–48; Chadwick,

Of relevance to our discussion is the church father's articulation of the *logos spermatikos* doctrine. Appealing to the complementary understanding of reason (λόγος) featured in the Stoic, Middle Platonist, and Johannine traditions—let us recall the opening passage of the gospel of St. John—Justin described how Christ (ὁ Λόγος τοῦ Θεοῦ) is the rational principle that gives order and meaning to the entire creation. He therefore proclaimed that whichever pagans had lived virtuously and arrived at accurate perceptions of reality—including the famous philosophers, Socrates and Heraclitus, as well as the lesser-known Gaius Musonius Rufus—were ultimately indebted to Christ, who implants the gift of reason within every human being.[6] According to the apologist, this gift has moral implications, its proper use resulting in a lifestyle consistent with that of the Logos Incarnate.[7]

It is significant that Justin did not repudiate his Greco-Roman heritage, choosing instead to appropriate various aspects of different philosophical traditions for the purposes of catechetical instruction and conversion. To draw and convince crowds in Palestine and Rome (and possibly Ephesus), the church father preserved not only the philosophical vocabulary that both he and they had inherited but even the customary cloak typically worn by the Hellenic seekers of wisdom—at least until he was arrested, tried, and executed in Rome with his disciples for refusing to offer sacrifices to the pagan gods.[8]

Early Church, 28–29. Justin addressed his *Apologies* to Marcus Aurelius and the similarly intolerant ruler, Antoninus Pius. See Justin Martyr, *First Apology* 1.1, 80; Minns and Parvis, "Introduction" to *Justin, Philosopher and Martyr*, 36–37.

6. Justin Martyr, *First Apology* 5.4 and 46.2–4, 90–91, 200–1; Justin Martyr, *[Pars Secunda]* τοῦ αὐτοῦ ἁγίου Ἰουστίνου φιλοσόφου καὶ μάρτυρος ἀπολογία ὑπὲρ Χριστιανῶν πρὸς τὴν Ῥωμαίων σύγκλητον A [i.e., *Second Apology*] 7(8).1, 7.3, 10.8, 13.3 and 13.5, 296–99, 312–13, 320–21. See also: Minns and Parvis, "Introduction" to *Justin, Philosopher and Martyr*, 61, 65–66; Baghos, "Hellenistic Globalisation and the Metanarrative of the Logos," 31; Barnard, *Justin Martyr*, 89; Tatakis, *Christian Philosophy in the Patristic and Byzantine Tradition*, 29.

7. Justin Martyr, *First Apology* 46.4, 200–1; Justin Martyr, *Second Apology* 7(8).1–2, 296–99.

8. Eusebius, *Ecclesiastical History* 4.18.6, 370–71; Justin Martyr, *Dialogue with Trypho* 1.2, 3. See also Minns and Parvis, "Introduction" to *Justin, Philosopher and Martyr*, 32–33; Barnard, *Justin Martyr*, 12–13; Halton, "Introduction to This Edition" of Justin Martyr, *Dialogue with Trypho*, xii. Three recensions of Justin's martyr act have been transmitted to us, the latest of which dates from the early-fifth century. See Musurillo, "Introduction" to *Acts of the Christian Martyrs*, xvii–xx. For a thorough assessment of the most authentic versions and their theological and cultural significance, see Baghos, "Apologetic and Literary Value of the *Acts of Justin*," 25–54.

The saint's mission did not instantly lead to a fusion between Christianity and Greco-Roman culture. It took another century and a half before St. Constantine the Great granted state protection to the church.[9] Nonetheless, his attitude was generally adopted by the faithful throughout the Greek East and Latin West, which likewise preserved his memory through the continued publication of his works, as well as in martyr acts, treatises, and the hymns of his feast day.[10] We are greatly indebted to Justin for his wise and nuanced approach, which helped justify the use of Greek philosophical concepts and terms for all later church fathers, especially in their development of Orthodox Christology and cosmology. Justin's lasting influence on the Greek Orthodox Church in particular—mediated through Byzantium—can be discerned today at the Holy Monastery of Great Meteoron located in Central Greece. Above the monastery's entrance doors there is an icon of the Lord, from whom proceeds a vine that ties together the prophets. Flanking the doors on either side are Justin and St. Paul accompanied by ancient Greek poets, philosophers, and historians. These include Homer, Thucydides, Aristotle, and Plato, in addition to Solon, Pythagoras, and Socrates. Each of the ancient figures carries a scroll featuring a passage from their works that points to Christ's incarnation and ministry.

There is much we can learn from Justin, and it is incumbent on us to both explore his writings and celebrate his feast day. What the church father undoubtedly expects from us is that we do not bury the unique talents that we have received from Christ (Matt 25:14–30; Luke 19:12–27), whether these be of a practical or contemplative nature. We must preach the gospel using whatever gifts the Lord has bestowed on us while displaying compassion towards all, even our enemies. In this secular age—where Christians are generally being persecuted, intellectually if not physically—we are often called to bear witness at the expense of our respective reputations. So long as we remember to pray to Justin and similar intercessors, we will surely find the strength to act accordingly. Furthermore, bearing in mind the great saint's behavior in his wider society and his written teachings, we must not be afraid of those aspects of secular culture that are compatible with the gospel—Christ is indeed the source of everything rational and noble in this world. It is therefore essential for us to seek common ground

9. Eusebius, *Ecclesiastical History* 10.1–4, 391–97.

10. *Calendar of Orthodox Saints and Feast Days*; Jerome of Stridon, *On Illustrious Men* 23, 43–46.

with unbelievers for the sake of mission, whether this be in relation to art and culture or the hard sciences. We certainly have a wonderful intercessor before Christ who will assist us in this undertaking, having dwelt in a world remarkably like our own and experienced many of the same challenges.

26

5

The Formative Value of Scripture

What We Can Learn from Sts. Athanasius the Great, Cyril of Alexandria, and Gregory of Nyssa

No one can deny the importance of formal education for interpreting the Scriptures. Contemporary, critical study of the Bible has positively contributed to the world's understanding of its literary and historical aspects. However, the status of divine revelation in hermeneutics has been unfairly marginalized within the academic context, as has the role of our tradition in the compilation of the Biblical canon.[1] As affirmed by Theodore G. Stylianopoulos, Scripture is a record of revelation reflecting the "interpreted experience and religious memory of God's people over many generations."[2] Truly, what we have with Scripture is God the Logos disclosing aspects of himself—and by extension the Father and the Holy Spirit—to us for our salvation via the written word, the greatest product of the human rational faculty which he inspired in the first place.[3] This twofold nature of Scripture as the "Word of God in human idiom" was central to the various interpretative methods of the church fathers, who discovered important allusions to the Holy Trinity even within the earliest books of the Old Testament, namely, Genesis and Exodus. More to the point, our saintly authorities considered

1. Stylianopoulos, *Scripture, Tradition, Hermeneutics*, 125–45.
2. Stylianopoulos, *Scripture, Tradition, Hermeneutics*, 33.
3. Stylianopoulos, *Scripture, Tradition, Hermeneutics*, 32–43.

all of Scripture from a Christocentric perspective and approached it out of a common soteriological concern for their respective congregations.[4]

We see such principles expounded upon by St. Athanasius of Alexandria—the confessor of the faith who battled the heresy of Arianism, which denied how Christ is coeternal and consubstantial with the Father—in his *Letter to Marcellinus*. In short, the letter was composed in response to a sick friend—likely a clergyman—seeking guidance in his exploration of the psalms.[5] Athanasius thus classified the numerous psalms and indicated how they are to be used in accordance with the different needs of the Christian life, ensuring the publication of his letter for the sake of posterity. The church father has therefore disclosed how we can use the Scriptures to praise and give thanks to God, seek repentance, endure hardship with hope, and confess our faith.[6] In the *Letter to Marcellinus* 1, Athanasius emphasizes that everything contained within the Bible is "inspired by God and profitable for teaching."[7] However, his focus in this work is primarily on the psalms, as he seeks to demonstrate how they constitute a synopsis of the Old Testament, a sacred garden containing wonders from the Mosaic law, the histories, and the prophets.[8] The saint has shared his conviction that the psalter allows its reciters to claim its divinely inspired words as their own, to be deeply moved in a manner incomparable.[9]

Athanasius maintained that Christians are not merely instructed to seek forgiveness within the psalms. Rather, they are given the proper words for repentance to commune with the Lord.[10] The psalter thus brings its reader into the life of God and places their prayers together with those of the saints, who intercede to the Paraclete on their behalf.[11] In the *Letter to Marcellinus* 31, Athanasius affirms, "recite and chant, without artifice, the things written just as they were spoken, in order for the holy men who supplied these, recognizing that which is their own, to join you in your

4. Stylianopoulos, *Scripture, Tradition, Hermeneutics*, 30–31, esp. 37.

5. Gregg, "Introduction" to Athanasius of Alexandria, *Life of Antony and the Letter to Marcellinus*, 21–25.

6. Nasuti, *Defining the Sacred Songs*, 112.

7. Athanasius of Alexandria, *Letter to Marcellinus* 1, 101.

8. Athanasius of Alexandria, *Letter to Marcellinus* 2, 102; Heine, *Reading the Old Testament with the Ancient Church*, 146–47.

9. Athanasius of Alexandria, *Letter to Marcellinus* 10–11, 108–9.

10. Heine, *Reading the Old Testament with the Ancient Church*, 147; Russell, *Making Your Life a Christian Life*, 44–45.

11. Russell, *Making Your Life a Christian Life*, 48.

prayer, or, rather, so that even the Spirit who speaks in the saints, seeing words inspired by him in them, might render assistance to us."[12] Athanasius is convinced that all of Scripture is united in and through the Holy Spirit: "for [He] is over all, and in each case with the distinction that belongs to it, each serves and fulfils the grace given to it, whether it is prophecy, or legislation, or the record of history, or the grace of the psalms."[13] Subsequently, the sacred songs are considered the means by which the sentiments of God's elect, described in a variety of ways in different literary contexts, are realized in the common believer.[14]

The existential import of Scripture was likewise emphasized by Athanasius' successor, St. Cyril of Alexandria, who tied it to not only worship and theology, but also asceticism. In short, Cyril was directly instructed by the cenobites of Egypt as a young man, having been advised by his uncle and bishop, Theophilus of Alexandria, to spend some time in their company in accordance with local custom.[15] Cyril associated with and advised the Egyptian monastic community throughout the remainder of his life, seeking its help to refute the heresy of Nestorius, i.e., the absurd notion that the person of Jesus and the Divine Logos are entirely distinct, each having a separate essence.[16]

Compared to modern exegetes, Cyril was less concerned with the philological dimension of Scripture, at least not for the purpose of literary criticism or historical reconstructionism. For instance, he engaged with the book of Isaiah primarily to illustrate the redemptive work of Christ for the gentiles as God and perfect man. Like Athanasius, Cyril maintained that Christ must be the interpretive lens through which to perceive both the Old and New Testaments, the purpose and goal of the entire Bible.[17]

12. Athanasius of Alexandria, *Letter to Marcellinus*, 31, 127.

13. Athanasius of Alexandria, *Letter to Marcellinus*, 9, 107.

14. Athanasius of Alexandria, *Letter to Marcellinus*, 10–11, 107–11.

15. McGuckin, *St. Cyril of Alexandria*, 3–4.

16. Cyril of Alexandria, *Cyril's Letter to the Monks of Egypt*, 245–61, esp. 249 n. 2. For a summary of the Nestorian controversy, see Russell, *Cyril of Alexandria*, 31–58. Cyril's positive legacy among the Eastern ascetics is evidenced in the alphabetical collection of their *Sayings*. Take, for instance, the story in which Abba Daniel praises Cyril for guiding a monk away from the false notion that the Old Testament figure of Melchizedek was the Son of God (rather than a type pointing to the latter as the high priest of the church). There is also the story in which Abba Isaac indicates that Cyril ordained his spiritual father, Motius, to the bishopric. See *Sayings of the Desert Fathers*, 54, 148–49.

17. Cyril of Alexandria, *Commentary on Isaiah*, 71; O'Keefe, "Christianizing Malachi," 140–41.

In his *Commentary on Isaiah*, the saint outlines the difficulties associated with the interpretation of Scripture, advising his flock that it is "filled with hidden meanings and is in travail with the predictions of divine mysteries." Cyril nonetheless exhorts his audience to identify and proceed through the literal and spiritual layers of each passage that it "might derive profit from every aspect of the text . . ."[18]

The influence of the monastic tradition on Cyril's interpretative framework is apparent in the prologue to his commentary. After acknowledging that his work may address spiritual themes which have already been examined at length by the saints, Cyril affirms that this does not discourage him from writing in the slightest. Instead, he declares that additional testimony can only serve to validate the truth. The church father asserts, "Accordingly, I have persuaded myself to overcome my diffidence in the conviction that the sweat and labour expended in a good project is better than a life of leisure."[19] This affirmation reflects a major principle of the desert fathers: that spiritual harmony results from hard work associated with the faith, however tedious it may seem. Interestingly, Cyril implies that intensive scholarly endeavors related to the Scriptures constitute practical asceticism, much like fasting or keeping vigil.[20]

Conditioned by different historical circumstances, the saints have faced their own unique challenges throughout the ages for the benefit of the faithful. Nevertheless, their works remain equally formative since they stem from genuine participation in the divine life. It inevitably follows that the writings of the learned hierarchs of the church, on the one hand, and the sayings and proverbs attributed to the masters of asceticism, on the other, often concern the same spiritual topics. Judging from his *Commentary on Isaiah*, Cyril presupposes a balance between experiential faith, intellectual understanding, and respect for the customs of the church. He implies that faith, reason, and ascetical effort are essential for understanding Scripture.[21] This should come

18. Cyril of Alexandria, *Commentary on Isaiah*, 71.

19. Cyril of Alexandria, *Commentary on Isaiah*, 72.

20. From this perspective, his attitude concerning hard work is consistent with that of Abba Isidore the Priest as recorded in the following aphorism attributed to St. Poeman: "Isidore, the presbyter in Scetis, once spoke to a group of monks and said, 'My brothers, isn't work the reason why we are here? But now I see that no work is done here. So I will take my cloak and go where there is work and so I shall find rest.'" *Desert Fathers: Sayings of the Early Christian Monks*, 63.

21. For a similar contention in relation to the patristic tradition generally, see Stylianopoulos, *New Testament*, 33, 80–100.

as no surprise given that he drew directly from the works of St. Jerome of Stridon—the ascetic and exegete par excellence—when composing his text. To be sure, both Jerome and Cyril maintained that that the aim of Scripture is to illustrate the Lord's saving activity, truth, and character as revealed in time.[22] The same can be said of St. Gregory of Nyssa, a near contemporary of Athanasius and fellow proponent of what has been termed the "Alexandrian school" of Biblical interpretation.

Like most church fathers affiliated with the masterful exegete, Origen, Gregory maintained that it was the task of the preacher to discern the literal, moral, allegorical, and spiritual sense of Scripture.[23] The Nyssen's command of the allegorical approach is evidenced in his *Life of Moses*, a much celebrated and detailed exposition of the book of Exodus, particularly the titular prophet's encounter with God on Mount Sinai. Let us therefore consider the latter half of the *Life of Moses*, in which the saint examines Exod 19–30.

Gregory begins by describing the trials, ascetic purification, and detachment from the senses required of the holy prophet Moses to contemplate divine realities.[24] He then discusses how the term "darkness" in Exod 20:21 signifies the incomprehensibility of the divine essence, which Moses was made aware of prior to engaging in the ascetic life.[25] Moreover, Gregory evaluates the way the prophet obtained mystical insight through contemplation of the created order.[26] He next evaluates the various features of the heavenly tabernacle which served as a prototype for Moses' earthly imitation (Exod 26), outlining how it symbolizes Christ whilst its contents represent the angles and the Holy Spirit, among other things.[27] In addition, Gregory suggests that the earthly tabernacle constructed by Moses and its surroundings denote the community of Christians and their love for one another.[28] The Nyssen also indicates how the dyed skin and hair coverings in the earthly tabernacle allude to the ascetic lifestyle, before revealing how

---

22. Russell, *Cyril of Alexandria*, 16, 70–71.

23. Simonetti, "Exegesis," 337.

24. Gregory of Nyssa, *Life of Moses* 152–61, 91–94.

25. Gregory of Nyssa, *Life of Moses* 162–66, 95–96.

26. Gregory of Nyssa, *Life of Moses* 167–69, 96.

27. Gregory of Nyssa, *Life of Moses* 170–81, 97–100.

28. Gregory of Nyssa, *Life of Moses* 184–86, 101–2.

its inner sanctuary (i.e., the "Holy of Holies") symbolizes divine realities beyond human understanding.[29]

We can see that Gregory embellishes Moses' experience on Mount Sinai to illustrate how the faithful can attain perfection. The prophet thus serves an image of the soul struggling to commune with God.[30] Yet Moses is also depicted as a contemplative ascetic who must acknowledge his ontological limitations and eliminate every preconceived notion that he has regarding the divine essence to avoid idolatry.[31] The Nyssen thus employs the term "darkness" to suggest that knowledge of God's essence is beyond human comprehension. However, the church father also affirms that St. John the Theologian first expressed this after having "penetrated the luminous darkness."[32] Hence, within the Nyssen's corpus, "the divine darkness implies two things at once: the unknowability of God's essence and the intimacy of God's presence to the soul embraced by what she cannot comprehend."[33]

It is apparent that Gregory maintained that the figures, events, and ritual items and practices recorded in Exod 19–30 foreshadowed those of the church. The Nyssen's desire to associate the Old Testament with the personal spiritualty and liturgical experience of the responder should come as no surprise given his conviction that the interpreter must go beyond the literal meaning of the text if it does not immediately inspire righteous conduct.[34] Gregory certainly does not deny the historical reality of Exodus in the *Life of Moses*.[35] Nevertheless, he employs an exegetical procedure known as ἀναγωγή which "elevates the letter of the text from the first level of literalness to the higher one of the spiritual signification."[36]

In summary, we should be suspicious of anyone who ignores the patristic contribution to hermeneutics. We must also eschew the prevalent preoccupation with the literary-historical method. As indicated by Sts. Athanasius, Cyril, and Gregory, every passage of Scripture has been composed with intention of transforming—not merely informing—the faithful.

---

29. Gregory of Nyssa, *Life of Moses* 187–88, 102–3.

30. Simonetti, "Vit Moys," 789.

31. Laird, "Darkness," 203.

32. Gregory of Nyssa, *Life of Moses* 163, 95.

33. Laird, "Darkness," 204; Gregory of Nyssa, *Life of Moses* 165, 95–96.

34. Simonetti, "Exegesis," 334.

35. Simonetti, "Vit Moys," 788.

36. Simonetti, "Exegesis," 335.

Having communed with the Word of God by means of worship and ascetical purification, the church fathers had a holistic approach when engaging with both the Old and New Testaments, which they treated as an organic whole. The saints properly exalted the authority and centrality of the whole Bible in the Christian life whilst maintaining an appropriate degree of freedom in their exegesis of any given book featured therein, concentrating on the spirit rather than the letter of the text. They were similarly pastorally motivated, mining and adapting the rich and hidden gems of Scripture for the purpose of drawing us closer to their ultimate inspiration, that is, our one true God subsisting in three Persons: Father, Son, and Holy Spirit.

6

St. Gregory of Nyssa on Asceticism and Spiritual Guidance

And if we recognize Christ as "sanctification," in whom every action is steadfast and pure, let us prove by our life that we ourselves stand apart, being ourselves true sharers of His name, coinciding in deed and not in word with the power of His sanctification.
—St. Gregory of Nyssa, *On Perfection*.[1]

St. Gregory of Nyssa was born to an aristocratic family in Cappadocia during the early fourth century. This was a turbulent time in the history of our church, when heretical sects descending from Arianism were continuing to deny our Lord Jesus Christ's equality with God the Father as concerns his divinity. Gregory—a younger brother of St. Basil the Great—proceeded through the classical education system typical of the age in the Eastern cities of Neocaesarea and Caesarea, acquiring masterful knowledge of oratory, multiple philosophical schools, and even medicine. Following in his father's footsteps, Gregory became a professional rhetorician while serving as a reader of the church. He also married a certain Theosebeia, at the same time maintaining a special reverence for monasticism and close contact with his family (most of which had pursued the angelic life by this stage). Gregory then heeded his brother Basil's call to become a presbyter in defense of the Orthodox faith (no doubt owing to his own spiritual experiences, including a vision of the Forty Martyrs of Sebaste).

1. Gregory of Nyssa, *On Perfection*, 103.

Gregory was soon elevated to the rank of bishop of the newly established see of Nyssa. However, owing to political contrivances on the part of the "Homoian" group of Arians, he was subjected to exile for several years. The confessor providentially returned to his bishopric where he took on the salvific mission of Basil in the East following the latter's repose. Gregory not only combatted the prevailing heresies in a manner reminiscent of Basil but also defended and built on his brother's written corpus, always referring to him with the utmost respect. He thus played an essential role in outlining the relationship between our Lord's human and divine natures on the one hand and that between the Father, the Son, and the Holy Spirit on the other. The church father also strove to establish ecclesial unity throughout Asia Minor, Arabia, and Jerusalem, as evidenced by his participation in a local Council of Antioch, in addition to the Second Ecumenical Council in Constantinople. Moreover, Gregory was a renowned pastor, preacher, and promoter of the veneration of the saints during his own lifetime.[2]

As revealed in his philosophical and spiritual works on the current and paradisal constitution of the human person—namely, *On the Making of Man* and *On the Soul and the Resurrection*—the Nyssen contributed to the Orthodox Church's conviction that we must rationally master our concupiscible and irascible appetites (i.e., our desire and anger). More precisely, he held that we must transform these drives by reorienting them from our selfish vices to the selfless virtues manifested by our Lord and Savior, precisely that we may be saved.[3] Gregory taught that this transformation leads to the restoration of the divine image (Gen 1:26–27) within us, which he claimed consists of "purity, freedom from passion, blessedness, alienation from all evil, and all those attributes of the like kind, which held to form in men the likeness of God . . ."[4] Amongst these qualities is liberty of choice, which the Nyssen termed *proairesis*.[5] The church father maintained that each of us is required to actively coordinate our *proairesis* and inclinations to the same noble ends to attain the Godlike existential mode intended for us by the Holy Trinity from the outset of creation.[6]

2. Maraval, "Biography of Gregory of Nyssa," 103–16.

3. For instance, the church father has spoken of the transformation of "anger" into "courage," "terror" into "caution," "fear" into "obedience," and "hatred" to "aversion from vice." Gregory of Nyssa, *On the Making of Man* 18.5, 408; Gregory of Nyssa, *On the Soul and the Resurrection*, 56–60.

4. Gregory of Nyssa, *On the Making of Man* 5.1, 391.

5. For more on this concept, see: Dal Toso, "Proairesis," 647–49.

6. Blowers, "Gentiles of the Soul," 64.

It is significant that, for Gregory, the self-mastery defined above cannot be achieved solely through the study of ascetical writings. Neither can it be accomplished in isolation. The church father insisted that asceticism requires the guidance of a spiritual elder who genuinely lives out the gospel. This is demonstrated in the twenty-third chapter of his treatise *On Virginity*, in which he encourages Christians who desire celibacy to: "search out a fitting guide and master of this way, lest, in their present ignorance, they should wander from the direct route . . ."[7] Gregory subsequently criticizes those who engage in ascetical practices entirely on their own, listing the various ways in which they fall. For instance, he asserts that some place false confidence in dreams while others fast excessively and tragically extinguish their lives.[8] In the subsequent chapter, the church father praises the fact that there are many saintly role models from amongst his own generation whom his readers generally—regardless of their marital status—can aspire to imitate and thus come to know Christ.[9] To be sure, the saint developed a timeless portrait of the ideal ascetic and spiritual guide, advising us as follows:

> If you see a man so standing between death and life, as to select from each helps for the contemplative course [. . .];—a man who remains more insensate than the dead themselves to everything that is found on examination to be living for the flesh, but instinct with life and energy and strength in the achievements of virtue, which are the sure marks of the spiritual life;—than look to that man for the rule of your life . . .[10]

The Nyssen's depiction of the eminent Orthodox role model is even more authoritative when we consider that it was directly influenced by Sts. Basil the Great and Macrina the Younger, the two greatest contributors to his Christian formation.[11] Basil certainly needs no introduction, being widely acknowledged within our church as the ideal pastor, theologian, monk, hierarch, and humanist. Our holy mother Macrina, however, is less known although equally important in the history of our tradition. In short, the blessed ascetic was the elder sister, childhood teacher, and spiritual guide of both Basil and Gregory. She was named after the pious siblings' heroic

---

7. Gregory of Nyssa, *On Virginity* 23, 369; Blowers, "Gentiles of the Soul," 63.

8. Gregory of Nyssa, *On Virginity* 23, 369.

9. Gregory of Nyssa, *On Virginity* 24, 369.

10. Gregory of Nyssa, *On Virginity* 24, 370.

11. Maraval, "Biography of Gregory of Nyssa," 104.

grandmother, a disciple of St. Gregory the Wonderworker (after whom the Nyssen was named) and brave survivor of the late-third/early-fourth century persecutions of the church. Yet Macrina also bore the name "Thekla" privately since her mother, St. Emmelia, had seen the eponymous martyr, virgin, and disciple of St. Paul the Apostle in a dream while pregnant with her. Following the death of her fiancé, Macrina chose not to marry and aided her widowed mother in raising the other children of the family. In her capacity as spiritual adviser, Macrina helped Emmelia bear the accidental death of her son, St. Naucratius, as well as establish a monastic community on the grounds of her estate with her serving-women.[12]

Gregory especially praised Macrina's fortitude and wisdom, as evidenced by *On the Soul and the Resurrection*, which consists in a dramatic dialogue between the two regarding the psychosomatic makeup of the human person and its eventual transfiguration through the grace of God. As evidenced by his Platonic representation of his sister, Gregory considered Macrina the Christian equivalent to Socrates. Such pronounced admiration for a woman on the part of a bishop of Late Antiquity, a man whom tradition considers a "Father of the Fathers," attests to the egalitarian aspect of Orthodoxy: that the state of holiness, including the divine knowledge which this entails, is open to all. Certainly, as early as the first chapter of the dialogue, Macrina manifests the signs of holiness articulated by Gregory in the above passage from *On Virginity*, admonishing him for experiencing grief upon seeing her mortally ill whilst appealing to the hope in the next life espoused by Paul (1 Thess 4:13).[13] The Nyssen's numerous writings thus remain relevant to our common experience as Orthodox Christians since they underscore the need for us to seek out spiritual masters who have denied themselves and therefore reveal what it means to know and love God. Gregory's own tremendous example demonstrates that we must also cultivate humility to recognize such teachers in the first place, whatever our respective talents and virtues may be.

12. Gregory of Nyssa, *Life of St. Macrina*, 163–91.

13. Gregory of Nyssa, *On the Soul and the Resurrection*, 27.

7

The Legacy of the Latin Fathers

Many of us are undoubtedly familiar with what has come to be known as the "Great Schism" of 1054. Whilst the categories of "Greek East" and "Latin West" may be said to have merit when applied to the divided churches in Europe from the beginning of the second millennium to the early modern period, it is important for us to consider that Rome and its various jurisdictions constituted a bastion of Orthodoxy—a bulwark of the one holy, catholic, and apostolic church—throughout the first thousand years following our Lord's ministry.[1] For this reason, there are a myriad of saints from regions such as Gaul (i.e., modern-day France), Italy, Britain, Ireland, Germany, and even Scandinavia within our Orthodox liturgical calendar, practically each day of every month.

His Eminence Archbishop Stylianos of Australia (of thrice-blessed memory) often used to summarize the first Christian millennium as an age of glory, a period in which the gospel was bravely disseminated by our spiritual forebears from Africa and Asia Minor to the Germanic and Celtic lands within the space of a few centuries. Thanks to the valiant efforts of men and women of the Latin world in full communion with those of Byzantium—bishops, monastics, missionaries, and even simple settlers—the checkerboard of pagan kingdoms that rose to power after the fall of the Western Roman Empire were gradually baptized into Christ and thus cleansed from their pagan vices, whilst their unique native charisms were

---

1. For a summary of the "Great Schism," see McGuckin, *Orthodox Church*, 20–23.

refined and properly revealed.[2] Take, for example, the intimate relationship with nature characteristic of the Celts, or the assertive and adventurous spirit of the Germanic peoples. Such admirable qualities were transformed by the church for the benefit of all humanity through the moral instruction stemming from its living encounter with the Risen Lord. Hence, such striking traits can be seen in their purest forms within the written lives of many Western saints, including those of Cuthbert the Wonderworker of Lindisfarne and Guthlac the Hermit of Crowland.

The conversion of the various Western peoples, and indeed their social welfare, was due to native Latin speakers in areas such as Italy and Gaul who managed to retain many literary and administrative forms of the Roman Empire even after the capture of the old capital during the fourth century. In the same way that the Greek East had its spiritual luminaries and exemplars regardless of its historical vicissitudes, so too did the Latin West, at least until 1054. For example, Byzantium consistently celebrated the Alexandrian and Cappadocian Fathers as great defenders of Orthodoxy against a range of heresies, including Arianism, which denied our Lord and Savior's equality with God the Father as concerns his divinity. Yet so did the Western adherents of the Orthodox Church throughout the first millennium, even adding profound theologians to this number such as St. Hilary of Poitiers. Hilary came to be known as *Malleus Arianorum*, that is, "Hammer of the Arians," by contending against the heretics and their imperial patrons, as well as "Athanasius of the West" due to his imitation of the renowned Alexandrian, whom he courageously defended.[3]

The fourth and fifth centuries of the Latin Orthodox Church produced some of the greatest minds and most loving hearts the world has ever known. This is especially true with respect to Sts. Ambrose of Milan, Jerome of Stridon, Augustine of Hippo, and Gregory the Great. The well-educated Ambrose first enjoyed fame as a just governor of the city of Milan, where he displayed tremendous proficiency in law and rhetoric. The people of Milan admired him so much for his prudence that they providentially

2. Gregory the Great was especially significant in the conversion of the Western kingdoms. For an overview of his missionary activity, see Ricci, "Gregory's Missions to the Barbarians," 29–56.

3. For the earliest account of Hilary's defence of Orthodoxy, see Sulpicius Severus, *Chronicles* 2.39, 2.42 and 2.45, 166–67, 169–70, 173–74. For a summary of the church father's life and works, see Williams, "Introduction" to Hilary of Poitiers, *Commentary on Matthew*, 3–10. His direct (and highly significant) contributions to Christian doctrine are available in English translation (as listed within the bibliography).

forced him to succeed the Arian bishop, Auxentius, after the latter's death; Ambrose having attended the episcopal election to prevent any violence from breaking out between the different factions.[4] Although he attempted to reject the appointment because of his humble rank as a catechumen, Ambrose graciously conceded to the wishes of the populace in order to restore Nicene Orthodoxy within the province, which he successfully accomplished through his influential *Exposition of the Christian Faith*.[5]

As bishop, Ambrose's generosity to the poor was such that he not only gave them all his personal property, but also sold the church's sacred vessels to pay ransoms for Christians that had been captured by barbarian invaders.[6] Moreover, the church father's conviction that Christ was the ultimate ruler of the earth was so authentic that he humbled Emperor Theodosius I for his massacre of certain rioters, barring the ruler from entering his cathedral and preventing him from partaking of the Eucharist until he displayed genuine repentance in public over the course of multiple months.[7] In addition, Ambrose displayed the gifts of wonderworking in his altruistic compassion, even calling a dead boy back to life through the grace of God.[8] He also enjoyed friendly correspondence with St. Basil the Great.[9]

Augustine of Hippo needs no introduction. His ardent love for the Lord and extreme humility are widely celebrated because of his *Confessions*, as well as his (near countless) treatises, sermons, letters, and biblical commentaries. The *Confessions* happen to constitute the first systematic autobiography and thorough exploration of the soul in the history of world literature. It is movingly framed within an earnest prayer to God, in which the church father narrates his fall and redemption in a manner that reflects the fate of wider humanity. In short, Augustine wrote his *Confessions* after certain rigorist and hardhearted heretics known as the Donatists intercepted and published a list of his former errors recorded by a certain cleric, chiefly, to tarnish his reputation and thereby silence his righteous criticisms of their failures. The saint responded to his critics—some of whom also came from within the church, having remembered his former errors and questioned

---

4. Paulinus, *Life of St. Ambrose* 2, 34–36. This life was composed by a direct disciple of Ambrose at the request of Augustine of Hippo.

5. Ambrose of Milan, *Exposition of the Christian Faith*, 201–314.

6. *Life of St. Ambrose* 9, 56; Ambrose of Milan, *De officiis* 2.70–71, 136–43.

7. *Life of St. Ambrose* 7, 46–48.

8. *Life of St. Ambrose* 8, 50.

9. Basil the Great, *To Ambrose, Bishop of Milan*, 42–45.

his ordination—by announcing to everyone in writing every major sin that he had committed until the moment of his conversion. This included his adherence to the fundamentally pagan religion known as Manichaeism in defiance of his holy mother, Monica.[10] Moreover, he wished to demonstrate to his admirers that whatever positive transformation he had accomplished in terms of character stemmed from God's mercy.[11]

Of particular importance is Augustine's account of his gradual transformation thanks to: the prayers of his saintly mother; the eloquent interpretation of the Scriptures and spiritual counsel offered by Ambrose; and, finally, Divine Providence, particularly upon hearing an account of simple soldiers who were compelled to become monks after learning the story of St. Antony the Great.[12] It is a great tragedy that certain people appeal to the later Western overemphasis on flawed aspects of Augustine's immense thought—which are, in fact, incredibly limited when considering his vast body of work—to discredit the saint, thus denying themselves an illustrious intercessor before God and essential model of virtue and piety, as emphasized by St. Photios the Great.[13] Undoubtedly, it is near impossible for the discerning Christian to read Augustine's description of the defining moment of his conversion—that is, the sudden burst of compunction which led him to read and internalize St. Paul's exhortation to "put on the Lord Jesus Christ" (Rom 13:14)—without being moved to tears.[14]

Jerome, who earned the title *Vir ecclesiasticus* or "Man of the Church," was granted such spiritual insight and intellectual charisms by the Lord that one cannot deny his attainment of the state of holiness. The church father was born in the city of Stridon on the border between Pannonia and Dalmatia, in what is now Bosnia and Herzegovina. He later went to Gaul to become a monk and soon returned to his native homeland to care for his siblings after their parents' repose. As a young man, he travelled to Rome, where he was first educated in the pagan classics, eventually studying theology in Trier. He later trained in Constantinople under St. Gregory the Theologian, whom he deeply cherished as a divinely inspired

---

10. Chadwick, "Introduction" to Augustine of Hippo, *Confessions*, xi–xii.

11. Pine-Coffin, "Introduction" to Augustine of Hippo, *Confessions*, 12.

12. Augustine of Hippo, *Confessions* 1.1, 3.12, and 8.6–12 (trans. Pine-Coffin), 22, 69–70, 166–79.

13. Photios the Great, *Mystagogy of the Holy Spirit* 65–71, 90–94.

14. Augustine of Hippo, *Confessions* 8.11–12, 175–79.

teacher, as demonstrated by his positive references to the Cappadocian within his written corpus.[15]

After returning to Rome, the church father soon became weary of the city's moral failings, which he boldly denounced. He eventually forsook Rome and ventured to the Holy Land where, living in a cave in Bethlehem near the site of our Lord's nativity, he became a defender of monks, an interpreter of Scripture, a formulator of doctrine, a chronicler of past saints, and a master translator, exercising his skill in Latin, Greek, Hebrew, and Chaldean.[16] Yet he likewise displayed great humility on the journey towards deification. This is verified, for instance, by his constant effort to curb any potential preference for style over content on the part of his more refined readers, chiefly by accusing himself for excessive interest in classical literature.[17] It is, indeed, quite striking that he never allowed his ascetical stamina or literary prowess—both of which were largely unparalleled—to hinder his relationship with Christ, his firm foundation, having once described himself as follows: "I am like the sick sheep that strays from the rest of the flock. Unless the Good Shepherd takes me on His shoulders and carries me back to His fold, my steps will falter, and in the very effort of rising my feet will give way."[18]

Gregory the Great proved to be one of the most influential people in history, having saved Western Europe from falling into chaos after the Lombard invasion of Italy and the ascension of various pagan and Arian kingdoms throughout the West. Gregory was born to an aristocratic family which had long since participated in the administration of the city of Rome; a family so pious that it produced a holy bishop for the prominent see, namely, Felix III. Gregory's mother, Sylvia, also became a saint, instilling profound moral and spiritual values in her gifted son from a young age. Gregory acquired the advanced literary-rhetorical education of the time, and it was hoped by his peers that he would eventually become a civil leader, but he instead chose to commit himself to Christ after the repose of his

15. See, for example, Jerome's summary of his teacher's career and writings. Jerome of Stridon, *On Illustrious Men* 117, 151–53.

16. For a brief biography of the church father, see Scheck, "Introduction" to Jerome of Stridon, *Commentary on Matthew*, 3–12.

17. See especially Jerome's account of the dream in which he saw the Lord accusing him of being a Ciceronian, rather than a Christian. Jerome of Stridon, *To Eustochium*, 166.

18. Jerome of Stridon, *To Theodosius and the Other Anchorites Living in Residence with Him* 2, 28.

father. Remarkably, he used his inheritance to establish no less than six monasteries, including one dedicated to the holy apostle Andrew, the First-Called, on the Caelian Hill. Gregory was nonetheless called by Pope Pelagius to serve the church in an administrative capacity, becoming a representative of the Roman see in Constantinople for several years, where he continued to live as a monk despite his many social responsibilities.[19] Tradition maintains that he was inspired by the Byzantine liturgies that he attended in the great city to establish what continues to be known as "Gregorian" chant. Additionally, through his spiritual fortitude, Gregory made the time to compose his *Moral Lessons on the Book of Job*, which is amongst the longest and most multifaceted writings by the church fathers.[20]

Following the repose of Pelagius, Gregory was unanimously elected bishop of Rome, an appointment which he attempted to flee for many months likely owing to his desire to retain the spiritual heights that he experienced in the state of contemplation. He eventually conceded to the wishes of the church when the Lord made him realize that even contemplation must be postponed for the sake of apostolic work and pastoral care when the laborers are few.[21] He lovingly guided the church and the wider society in this capacity for over a decade, helping Rome survive disastrous famine and plague; the latter by zealously mobilizing his flock in prayer. What is more, Gregory established the first mission to the Anglo-Saxons, which he entrusted to the industrious and influential apostle, St. Augustine of Canterbury.[22] All the while the great saint suffered from debilitating fevers and pain caused by untreatable gout, thus teaching us that faith

19. There are at least three traditional Christian accounts of Gregory's life ranging from the late seventh to early ninth centuries (two of which are available in English translation). *Earliest Life of Gregory the Great by an Anonymous Monk of Whitby*; Bede the Venerable, *History of the English Church and People* 2.1, trans. Leo Sherley-Price (Harmondsworth, Middlesex: Penguin Books, 1955), 93-99; Paul the Deacon, *Sancti Gregorii Magni Vita*. The renowned editor and translator Bertram Colgrave wrote a useful summary of the church father's formation, career, and historical context. See Colgrave, "Introduction" to *Earliest Life of Gregory the Great*, 19–31.

20. Marcus Adriaen has produced a critical edition consisting of three volumes (complete details within the bibliography).

21. Although Gregory experienced grief in being taken from his contemplative life within the context of a monastery, he nonetheless went on to underscore the necessity of heeding the call to ordination and elevation, even when one may be inclined to refuse on account of humility. See: Gregory the Great, *Registrum epistolarum* 1.5 (PL 77, 448A–450C); Gregory the Great, *Pastoral Care* 1.6–7, 32–34.

22. For more on Gregory and Augustine's tremendous mission to the Anglo-Saxons, see Bede the Venerable, *History of the English Church and People* 1.23–2.3, 66–102.

can ultimately eclipse every illness, allowing us to achieve wonders for the church whatever our physical condition may be.[23]

On a related note, it is important for us to bear in mind that the see of Rome was for the most part Orthodox throughout the first millennium, producing many eminent theologians, among them Sts. Theodore and Martin the Confessors. In imitation of their predecessor and significant expositor of Christ's two natures, St. Leo the Great, the fearless hierarchs contended against the Monothelite heresy, whose proponents denied our Lord's human will to establish unity with the Monophysites. In an outstanding collaboration with St. Maximus the Confessor and his monastic cohort from Byzantium, Theodore and Martin defied both a heretical emperor and patriarch of Constantinople, emphasizing that the Incarnate Lord must have a human will if we are to be saved (remembering that Christ graciously healed whatever he assumed in his humanity).[24] Theodore, Martin, and Maximus were eventually vindicated when the emperor and hierarchs of Constantinople returned to the Orthodox faith. This may largely be attributed to St. Agatho of Rome, who reiterated their position at the Sixth Ecumenical Council.[25]

We could also discuss the influential monks and miracle workers of the Late Antique and early medieval Latin West—including Sts. John Cassian, Martin of Tours, and Benedict of Nursia—who transmitted the spiritual experience of the hermits and cenobites of Egypt, Asia Minor, and Mesopotamia to the forests of the European Continent, and, in turn, the Irish bogs and English marshlands.[26] For now, let us content ourselves by

23. For a recent assessment of the church father's affliction, see Hosler, "Gregory the Great's Gout," 11–32.

24. For the earliest accounts of the suffering endured by Martin and Maximus, see *Record of the Trial, Dispute at Bizya,* and *Commemoration,* in *Maximus the Confessor and His Companions,* 48–74, 75–119, 148–71. For a summary of the Monothelite controversy, and the central role of Theodore, Martin, and Maximus in the defence of the doctrine of the Lord's two wills, see Allen and Neil, "Introduction" to *Maximus the Confessor and His Companions,* 1–21.

25. *Sixth Ecumenical Council—The Third Council of Constantinople, A.D. 680–681,* 328–41.

26. For evidence of the Continental transmission of the Byzantine monastic experience, see John Cassian, *Conferences; Sulpicius Severus: Writings,* 101–251; Gregory the Great, *Dialogues* 2, 55–110. The *Life of St. Benedict* constitutes the entire second part of Gregory's celebrated *Dialogues* on the saints of Italy. Interestingly, the latter became known within the Byzantine tradition as "the Dialogist" owing to the popularity of this work in Greek translation (made by Bishop Zacharias of Rome, the last of the "Greek popes," c. 741–752). Louth, "Gregory the Great in the Byzantine Tradition," 343–58, esp.

reflecting on the fact that we have a similar calling to our Latin Fathers and their immediate followers, primarily, to assimilate and internalize the spiritual treasures first developed in Byzantium and subsequently transmit these to our Western compatriots, enriching them through our own asceticism and prayer. Furthermore, we must remember that we have numerous intercessors before Christ whose writings are widely accessible in English translation, and whose legacies needs to be re-examined in the light of Orthodoxy (which rightly claims the genuine preservation of their general spirituality). Let us therefore join our loving Latin Fathers in celebrating our Lord's victory over death, proudly exclaiming with them: "*Christus resurrexit! Vere resurrexit!*" (Christ has risen! Truly he has risen!)

344.

8

St. Martin of Tours, Our Witness to Christ, and His Disciple, Sulpicius Severus

THERE IS SO MUCH that we can say in relation to the holy fathers and mothers of the Latin West, the wondrous saints who flourished in the European Continent and the British Isles before the "Great Schism" of 1054. In the previous chapter, I discussed how much we can gain in reclaiming the legacy of the valiant martyrs, ascetics, missionaries, and clergymen who dwelt in the West during the first millennium. We may uncover, for example, their literary, artistic, and administrative prowess, their apostolic fearlessness, their mystical insight, and, most importantly, their perfect love for God and neighbor. To this end, we can examine the lives of great saints like Cyprian of Carthage, Benedict of Nursia, and Brigit of Kildare. Yet I am compelled to limit this discussion to one figure who is dear to me personally, and whose experience became paradigmatic for our Western Christian forebears throughout the Middle Ages, namely, St. Martin of Tours.

I will not be examining the phenomenon of martyrdom per se, at least not what has come to be known as "red" martyrdom, the torture and execution for the sake of the Lord and his gospel suffered by Cyprian and similar figures. Rather, I will be discussing an eminent example of "white" martyrdom, a notion first developed by St. Athanasius of Alexandria in his life of St. Antony the Great, and which Evagrius of Antioch transmitted to the West through his Latin translation of this celebrated work. To be more precise, ascetic renunciation and labors, including vigils and contemplation, as well as the preservation of one's chastity, were considered forms of martyrdom throughout the Greek East and Latin West by the fourth century; together, these practices constituted a daily death which led to a new life in Christ. The popularity of this perception had as much to do with missionary work and pilgrimage on the part of holy ascetics as it did the translation of key ascetical and hagiographical works from Greek into Latin, including the *Sayings of the Desert Fathers* by the hand of St. John Cassian, and original compositions inspired by the former, such as St. Jerome of Stridon's *Life of St Paul the Hermit*.[1] To be sure, the Eastern and Western ascetics—beginning with Paul and Antony—likewise hoped to imitate the martyrs, whom they believed shared in Christ's triumph over sin and death as a result of their complete detachment from secular interests. Because of the physical and spiritual struggles which they encountered in their respective rural and wild locales, the first anchorites and cenobites were highly extolled by the church. It was believed that their prayers facilitated both ecclesial and civil welfare, a deep conviction still prevalent amongst us Orthodox.[2]

Moving on to our subject, Martin was born to pagan parents in Sabaria, capital city of the Roman province of Pannonia, in either 316 or 336 AD. He was raised in Pavia, Italy, where his father served as a Roman military tribune. Martin was in fact forced by his father to serve in the imperial army at the age of fifteen, that he might be deterred from his growing commitment to the Orthodox Christian faith, especially his interest in the eremitic life.[3] Martin was stationed in the Roman province of Gaul until one day, at the gates of the city of Amiens, he met a poor man waiting naked by the road, seeking alms. By this point, Martin's clothing had been reduced to his armor and cloak thanks to his continued commitment to Christ, best manifested in his humility, poverty, and charity. It was the middle of a harsh winter when many had been perishing from the cold. All who passed by the pauper as he pleaded for compassion chose to ignore him. Martin, however, already being filled with the grace of God, saw that this circumstance had been providentially arranged to test his virtue. Having already devoted the rest of his clothing to similar purposes, he drew his sword and cut his cloak in two. The young soldier then gave one part to the poor man,

---

1. Stancliffe, "Red, White and Blue Martyrdom," 30–31.

2. Chadwick, *Early Church*, 177; Ward, "Introduction" to *Desert Fathers*, viii.

3. Sulpicius Severus, *Vita Sancti Martini episcopi* [i.e., *Life of Martin*] 2.1–8, 96–97. All translations from Burton's edition featured in this book are my own. See also Mertens, *Old English Lives of St Martin of Tours*, 5–7.

modestly dressing himself with the other. Some of the bystanders began to laugh at the now awkward figure of Martin whilst others felt great shame, realizing that they might have easily clothed the pauper without stripping themselves in the freezing cold. That night, deep in sleep, Martin beheld our Lord and Savior, Jesus Christ, accompanied by the angels, clothed in the part of the cloak which he had given to the poor man. Martin was bidden to look attentively upon the Lord, to recognize the garment which he had generously bestowed at the city gates, with Christ proudly exclaiming that it was he who had been clothed by Martin, a mere catechumen, in accordance with his exhortation in Matt 25:40.[4]

This vision of Christ had such a profound effect on Martin that he immediately sought baptism, eventually forsaking his military career, and seeking out the profound theologian, St. Hilary of Poitiers, his future spiritual father. After many years in asceticism in Italy and Gaul, in perfect obedience to Hilary and Christ, Martin became so popular amongst the laity that he was elected bishop of Tours, his ordination probably taking place on 4 July 371.[5] On 8 November 397, Martin reposed in the city of Candes in Gaul whilst on a tour of his diocese at the age of 81 or 61 depending on the chronology. He was buried in Tours three days later. His feast is thus celebrated amongst the Orthodox traditions alternately on November 11 or 12.[6]

It is noteworthy that the wider Roman world was beginning to abandon paganism and embrace the Christian faith by Martin's time. Thanks to the heroic efforts of many bishops, most towns and their immediate vicinities were being converted to Orthodoxy throughout Egypt, Mesopotamia, Asia Minor, and the European Continent. Interestingly, Martin was amongst the first to venture out to the Western rural communities, where Roman and Celtic pagan beliefs were still quite prevalent.[7] This does not imply that the church attempted to displace the old ways entirely. Indeed, the traditional Roman civic institutions throughout the West were increasingly being challenged by Germanic tribes during this period, and it was the church which valiantly managed to preserve the positive cultural legacy of the Roman

4. Sulpicius Severus, *Life of Martin* 3.1–5, 96–99.

5. Sulpicius Severus, *Life of Martin* 9.1–7, 104–5; Mertens, *Old English Lives of St Martin of Tours*, 6, 11–12.

6. Sulpicius Severus, *Epistula secunda, ad Aurelium diaconum* [i.e., *Letter to Aurelius the Deacon*] 1–19, 324–35. See also Mertens, *Old English Lives of St Martin of Tours*, 6, 14.

7. Sulpicius Severus, *Life of Martin* 13.1–15.4, 108–13; McSherry, *Outreach and Renewal*, 106.

Empire even after the fall of the old capital; specifically, those Christians who drew upon the ancient poets, prose writers, and rhetoricians to disseminate the gospel to their wider society. Each of these authors has made an indelible contribution to the Orthodox and wider Western literary canons, amongst whom is Martin's beloved disciple, Sulpicius Severus.

Sulpicius Severus was born around the year 360. He came from a distinguished family in Aquitanian Gaul, eventually acquiring a thorough literary-rhetorical education at Bordeaux for the purpose of becoming a lawyer. Sulpicius gained some renown in this vocation before marrying the daughter of a noblewoman named Bassula. Upon the early death of his wife, Sulpicius began to embrace Christian asceticism together with his mother-in-law, receiving baptism in 390 with his friend, Paulinus. Both men foreswore their riches and secular fame, Suplicius having already made the acquaintance of Martin by this point. Paulinus was soon ordained a priest in Barcelona, subsequently moving to the Campanian town of Nola in southern Italy where he was elevated to the rank of bishop. Paulinus managed to maintain his friendship with Sulpicius, eventually becoming recognized as a saint within our church.[8]

After spending some time at Eluso (modern Elsonne, near Toulouse), Sulpicius retired with Bassula to a country estate known as Primulia-cum—likely near Beziers or Perigueux—which he developed into a monastic community. The fifth-century presbyter and historian, Gennadius of Marscilles, revealed that Suplicius was at some point ordained to the priesthood. Moreover, the historian affirmed that Sulpicius, advanced in years, fell victim to a common heresy of the time known as Pelagianism, which falsely proclaimed that humanity could attain perfection without the assistance of divine grace. This may account for why he has not been enrolled into the calendar of saints. However, it is important to note that Sulpicius earnestly repented according to Gennadius. More precisely, to remedy the loquaciousness which he felt had led to his fall, Sulpicius maintained absolute silence until his repose, which was likely between c. 411–420. One can imagine that that this was a severe form of penance for Sulpicius given the joy that he took in having conversations throughout his life; first as a legal orator, then as the leader of a monastic community in which it was his custom to vigorously discuss the lives of the saints.[9]

---

8. Peebles, "Introduction" to *Sulpicius Severus*, 80–81; Mertens, *Old English Lives of St Martin of Tours*, 14–15

9. Peebles, "Introduction" to *Sulpicius Severus*, 81–83.

At any rate, it is important to note that Martin appointed Suplicius as his major historical witness. This is evidenced, for instance, by their first encounter, in which Martin washed Sulpicius' feet in a manner echoing our Lord's same action towards his disciples at the Mystical Supper. More precisely, this humble service on the part of the saint suggests that he perceived Suplicius as one who would carry on his legacy after his ascension to heaven.[10] Moreover, Martin's affection for Sulpicius is suggested by the fact that he chose to reveal himself to the latter in a dream at the very moment in which his soul was being called to God.[11]

Sulpicius has related the conversion, mission, and repose of Martin in multiple works representing different genres, namely: a conventional life (c. 396–397), three surviving epistles (c. 397–404), and certain dialogues (c. 404).[12] Sulpicius' depiction of Martin is most nuanced within the *Dialogues*, in which he has explicitly likened the monastic bishop to his Byzantine counterparts. The *Dialogues* are essentially a stylized version of a discussion on Martin held between Sulpicius, a fellow disciple named Gallus, and their friend, Postumianus at Primuliacum.[13] In short, the *Dialogues* initially feature Postumianus as the principal narrator as he seeks to discover more about Martin's heroic feats whilst at the same time relating wonders involving Eastern ascetics that he has witnessed and heard about on a recent tour of Egypt and Palestine. Gallus then takes on the responsibility of describing Martin's accomplishments beyond those featured in Sulpicius' life.[14] Whilst Postumianus and Gallus serve as the

10. Sulpicius Severus, *Life of Martin* 25.1–8, 124–27; Tornau, "Intertextuality in Early Latin Hagiography," 165–66.

11. Sulpicius Severus, *Letter to Aurelius the Deacon* 1–6, 324–27.

12. For more on the purpose of these works, as well as their respective structures and occasions, see: Jacques Fontaine and Nicole Dupré, "Introduction" to *Gallus: Dialogues sur les «vertus» de saint Martin*, 17–96; Peebles, "Introduction" to *Sulpicius Severus*, 86–89; Goodrich, "Introduction" to *Sulpicius Severus*, 8–20; Burton, "Introduction" to *Sulpicius Severus' Vita Martini*, 4–6; Mertens, *Old English Lives of St Martin of Tours*, 14–31; Stancliffe, *St. Martin and His Hagiographer*, 71–107. For a thorough exploration of the chronology and historicity of the life in particular, see Fontaine and Dupré, "Introduction" to *Gallus*, 171–310; Burton, "Introduction" to *Sulpicius Severus' Vita Martini*, 9–25. For a comparative analysis of the chronology of Martin's life as presented by Sulpicius and St. Gregory of Tours, see Stancliffe, *St. Martin and His Hagiographer*, 111–33.

13. Clare Stancliffe identified Postumianus with the same figure that Paulinus recommended to Sulpicius by letter. Stancliffe, *St. Martin and His Hagiographer*, 49.

14. Burton, "Introduction" to *Sulpicius Severus' Vita Martini*, 4–5; Peebles, "Introduction" to *Sulpicius Severus*, 87–89; Goodrich, "Introduction" to *Sulpicius Severus*, 17–20. Citing Karl Suso Frank, Mertens incorrectly perceived the *Dialogues* as a defense

major speakers within the *Dialogues*, Sulpicius ultimately takes credit for their composition and theological themes.

Sulpicius' purpose in composing these works, collectively referred to as the *Martiniana*, was to present his subject as the ideal Christian, a source of inspiration and consolation for clergy and laity alike. In the *Life of Martin* 1, Sulpicius asserts that he thinks it "worthwhile" (*operae pretium*) to write down "the life of a most holy man" (*vitam sanctissimi viri*) so that his audience is encouraged towards "true wisdom, and heavenly warfare, and Godlike virtue" (*veram sapientiam et caelestem militiam divinamque virtutem*).[15] However, it has come to light through recent scholarship that Sulpicius' motivation was also polemical. To be more exact, Sulpicius intended to replace the pagan religious and moral values of Roman society—especially military valor and imperial authority—with the Christian virtue of humility.[16] He thus continued the work of his subject, who was amongst the first conscientious objectors in history.

It is noteworthy that Sulpicius directly challenged the prevailing Greco-Roman literary values, employing Latin rhetoric to highlight Martin's unique Christian qualities. Sulpicius emphasizes from the outset of the Life that he has no intention of ensuring a lasting legacy for himself; unlike the classical authors, he prioritizes the eternal life that may be acquired through the commemoration and imitation of a holy person.[17] This is despite the fact that he had extensive knowledge of the pagan classics, the Scriptures, and numerous martyrologies and hagiographies, including Evagrius' translation

---

of Western monasticism against that of the East, with Martin as a foil to the latter. This presupposes that Sulpicius perceived the two traditions as fundamentally at odds, yet his reiteration of Postumianus' positive discussion of the Eastern ascetics (including his own admission that their deeds are holy) proves that this certainly was not the case. As noted above, the hagiographer consistently drew on Eastern sources to depict his subject. Subsequently, it is apparent that Sulpicius intended to present Martin as part of the same tradition although worthy of more praise than many of his Eastern counterparts since he managed to perform the same feats despite the hostility that he encountered from jealous critics numbered amongst the Gallic clergy. See Sulpicius Severus, *Gallus sive Dialogi de virtutibus sancti Martini* [i.e., *Dialogues*] 1.24.1–26.8, 28.

15. "Therefore, what I am about to do seems to me worthwhile, supposing that I will have written down completely the life of a most holy man that is soon going to be, by means of example, for others; so that readers will be spurred on by all means toward true wisdom, and heavenly warfare, and Godlike virtue." Sulpicius Severus, *Life of Martin* 1.6, 94.

16. Bequette, "Sulpicius Severus' *Life of Saint Martin*," 56–78.

17. Sulpicius Severus, *Life of Martin* 1.1–8, 94.

of the *Life of Antony*.[18] Indeed, Sulpicius consciously based the epilogue of the *Life of Martin* on that found within the *Vita Antonii* as concerns its structure and grammar.[19] Subsequently, it is highly likely that such nuanced adaptation of the *Life of Antony* on the part of Sulpicius influenced his thinking more generally, hence his modesty, which should not be dismissed as a mere literary trope. The influence of this celebrated text also accounts for his depiction of practical asceticism and contemplation as the means by which Martin arrived at union with Christ.

In the *Life of Martin* 2, Sulpicius describes his subject's birth in Illyria and early life in Italy.[20] After relating that Martin was first a soldier and military tribune during the reigns of Constantius and Julian the Apostate, the hagiographer turns to the topic of his subject's youth. He affirms that the saint chose to become a Christian at the age of ten despite the protests of his pagan parents.[21] It is significant that Sulpicius asserts that Martin set out to become an ascetic in the wilderness when he was twelve years old but was prevented from doing so on account of the weakness characteristic of his age.

With respect to Martin's formation, the hagiographer does not provide an account of the saint's education, emphasizing instead his practical virtues as a soldier and catechumen.[22] Later, in the twenty-fifth chapter, Sulpicius marvels at the eloquence displayed by Martin as a bishop even though he had been "an unlearned man" (*homo illitteratus*).[23] This indicates that the ascetic received no formal training in either rhetoric or theology.

18. Stancliffe, *St. Martin and His Hagiographer*, 55–70; Burton, "Introduction" to *Sulpicius Severus' Vita Martini*, 25–81; Peebles, "Introduction" to *Sulpicius Severus*, 84–86; Goodrich, "Introduction" to *Sulpicius Severus*, 6–8; Mertens, *Old English Lives of St Martin of Tours*, 17–19; Tornau, "Intertextuality in Early Latin Hagiography," 158–66.

19. Notwithstanding their similarities, Tornau emphasised that the *Life of Martin* cannot be reduced to a mere copy or imitation of that concerning Antony. Tornau, "Intertextuality in Early Latin Hagiography," 161–62. For an exploration of the various features common to both works (and saints' lives generally during Late Antiquity), see: McCulloh, "Confessor Saints and the Origins of Monasticism," 21–32.

20. Sulpicius Severus, *Life of Martin* 2.1–4, 96.

21. Sulpicius relates that Martin eventually converted his mother whilst still a young monk, having been inspired by God in a dream to preach in his native homeland. Sulpicius Severus, *Life of Martin* 5–6, 109–12.

22. Sulpicius Severus, *Life of Martin* 2.5–4.9, 96–98.

23. "It is a marvellous thing that not even this charism had been lacking from an unlearned man." Sulpicius Severus, *Life of Martin* 25.8, 126.

Regarding his subject's practical virtues as a solider and catechumen, Sulpicius states that Martin continued to live as a rigid ascetic, even treating his sole servant as his master, humbling himself by cleaning the latter's boots.[24] The hagiographer emphasises Martin's "kindness" (*benignitas*), "love" (*caritas*), "patience" (*patientia*), "humility" (*humilitas*), and "temperance" (*frugalitas*) towards his fellow soldiers,[25] before describing how he tended "the suffering" (*laborantes*), "the distressed" (*miseri*), "the very poor" (*egentes*) and "the naked" (*nudi*). Interestingly, Sulpicius affirms that Martin kept "nothing for himself from his payments for his military service except his daily food."[26] These virtues represent practical asceticism in the tradition of the desert fathers, with most constituting individual chapters in the systematic collections of the latter's *Sayings*.[27]

In the *Life of Martin* 6, Sulpicius relates how the Arians persecuted his mentor during his missionary tour of Illyria. The hagiographer affirms that Martin returned to Italy and settled in Milan, where he established his first monastery.[28] According to Sulpicius, the ascetic was further harassed by the city's Arian bishop, Auxentius. Besides the hagiographer's testimony that Martin was in fact a confessor for the faith—that is, one who was tortured for Christ and his gospel, yet not to the point of death—the hagiographer's description of Martin's consequent withdrawal from the monastery to the island of Gallinara off the coast of Albenga, Italy, is of relevance to our discussion.[29] Sulpicius states that the saint lived at this remote location for

24. Sulpicius Severus, *Life of Martin* 2.5, 96.

25. "Great was that man's kindness/mercy with respect to his comrades, astonishing [his] love/esteem, and also, in truth, [his] patience and humility were beyond human measure. For instance, it is not necessary that the [quality of] temperance within him be commended; he practised it in such a manner so that, already at that time, he might be considered not a solider, but a monk." Sulpicius Severus, *Life of Martin* 2.7, 96.

26. "Of course, he was attending to those who were suffering, offering assistance to those in distress, feeding the very poor, clothing the naked, keeping nothing for himself from his payments for his military service except his daily food." Sulpicius Severus, *Life of Martin* 2.8, 96.

27. See the following chapters from the Greek and Latin systematic collections listed within the bibliography: "Περὶ ἀγάπης/*De charitate*" (17), "Περὶ ἀνεξικακίας/*De patientia*" (16), "Περὶ ταπεινοφροσύνης/*De humilitate*" (15), "Περὶ ἐγκρατείας καὶ ὅτι οὐ μόνον ἐπὶ βρωμάτων ταύτην παραληπτέον ἀλλὰ καὶ τῶν λοιπῶν τῆς ψυχῆς κινημάτων/*De continentia*" (4).

28. Sulpicius Severus, *Life of Martin* 6.4, 100–2.

29. Sulpicius Severus, *Life of Martin* 6.5–6, 102. The island's appellation stems from its native birds (*gallinae rusticae*). See Peebles, *Sulpicius Severus*, 112 n. 5.

some time on a diet of herb roots until he mistakenly ate the poisonous hellebore plant. The author asserts that Martin would have died had he not immediately resorted to prayer, through which he was healed.[30]

In the above story, Sulpicius tacitly presents his subject in an Edenic state that anticipates his future vocation as a redeemer of creation. Martin can survive in the wilderness on a diet of plants and is not permitted to perish owing to his commitment to God's law, here signified by orthodox doctrine.[31] The passage subtly evokes Gen 2:16–17, in which Adam is told that he will be able to live on every tree in the garden of paradise except that containing the knowledge of good and evil. A thorough analysis of the Tree of Knowledge is not necessary here. May it suffice to state that Sulpicius, in his summation of salvific history from the act of creation to his own time (known as his *Chronicles*), was content with interpreting the tree as the single law upon which Adam and Eve's residing in paradise depended. Unsurprisingly, his interpretation of Scripture is entirely consistent with that of Athanasius, whose work he knew through translation.[32]

30. Cf. Sulpicius Severus, *Dialogues* 1.15.2, in which Postumianus describes the anchorites of the deserts of Egypt who relied on the same food. *Dialogues* 1.15.2, 162. Interestingly, Postumianus relates the story of an anchorite who lived in the wilderness near Syene (modern Assuam) and had, as a novice, accidently ingested a poisonous herb root. To recover from the effects of the poison, and later distinguish between edible and dangerous roots, the anchorite appealed to an ibex. The cooperation of this creature presupposes a certain degree of holiness on the part of the ascetic. *Dialogues* 1.16.1–3, 166–68; Peebles, *Sulpicius Severus*, 183 n. 1.

31. Burton identified a typological connection between Martin, the prophet Elijah, the prophet Elisha, and St. John the Baptist in the depiction of the coarse food. More precisely, the scholar affirmed that Martin's consumption of the hellebore and other plants' roots is reminiscent of John's diet of locusts and wild honey (Matt 3:4; Mark 1:6), as well as Elijah's being fed by ravens and angels (3 Kgs 17:4–6, 19:5–8 LXX). Furthermore, Martin's neutralisation of the poisonous effects of the hellebore evokes that of Elisha with respect to wild gourds (4 Kgs 4:38–41 LXX). Burton, "Introduction" to *Sulpicius Severus' Vita Martini*, 33.

32. Sulpicius perceives paradise (*paradisus*) as distinct from "our land" (*nostram terram*) in his *Chronicles* 1.1, as in the case of Athanasius. It is noteworthy that Athanasius defines paradise as the saints' participation in God the Word owing to their preservation of the divine image (Gen 1:26–27). Drawing on Wis 6:18, Athanasius emphasises that the immortality characteristic of paradise can be reattained through contemplation and obedience. The church father thus identifies paradise as a distinct *topos* owing to a particular *tropos* (i.e., mode of being). The same can be said of Sulpicius as evidenced by his depiction of Martin. Sulpicius Severus, *Chronicorum* [i.e., *Chronicles*] 1.1, 92; Athanasius of Alexandria, *Incarnation of the Word of God* 1.3–4, 27–30. For a summary of the positive reception of Athanasius by the early Latin Fathers (specifically Hilary, Ambrose, Jerome, Augustine, and St. Leo the Great), see Weinandy and Keating, *Athanasius and*

Sulpicius has clearly depicted Martin as having advanced in the spiritual life through prayer, otherwise termed "contemplation." As a matter of fact, Sulpicius depicts Martin in a state of prayer numerous times throughout his works. Most of Martin's prayers constitute petitions, namely to: (i) heal or resurrect the faithful; (ii) ward off or pacify hostile forces (especially the devil); and (iii) dramatically abolish pagan places of worship, thereby converting the people of Gaul.[33] Of particular relevance is Sulpicius' affirmation that "Never did any hour and a moment go by in which he might not be either concentrating on prayer or diligently pursuing his reading; however, even during the act of reading, or if he was doing something else by chance, he never released his heart/mind from prayer."[34] Similarly, within his *Letter to Bassula*, the hagiographer emphasises that Martin, even as he suffered from the violent fever that led to his repose, spent the night "in prayers and vigils" (*in orationibus et uigiliis*).[35] Martin's desire for solitude to pray is especially evident in the tenth chapter of the life, where Sulpicius describes his quality of life as a bishop.[36] The hagiographer affirms that when Martin took on the episcopal role in Tours,

> [t]he same humility was in his heart, the same poverty was in his vesture; and so, full of authority and grace, he fulfilled the office of a bishop, yet not that he might forsake the resolution and virtue of a monk. Therefore, for some time he made use of a cell close to the church; then, when he was not able to bear the restlessness of those who were frequently visiting him, he set up for himself a monastery approximately two miles outside of the city.[37]

His Legacy, 74–77.

33. Sulpicius Severus, *Life of Martin* 6.6, 7.3–6, 10.6–7, 14.4, 22.1 and 26.3, 102, 107, 110, 120, 126; Sulpicius Severus, *Epistula prima, ad Eusebium* 13, 322; Sulpicius Severus, *Epistula tertia, Sulpicius Severus Bassulae parenti venerabili salutem* [i.e., *Letter to Bassula*] 14, 340; Sulpicius Severus, *Dialogues* 2.4.7, 3.2.5, 3.8.7, 3.9.1 and 3.15.5, 236, 294, 320, 322, 352.

34. Sulpicius Severus, *Life of Martin* 26.3, 127.

35. "Passing the night in prayers and vigils, he forced his exhausted limbs to obey his soul, as he lay down on that noted bed of his, in ashes and sackcloth." Sulpicius Severus, *Letter to Bassula* 14, 340.

36. Sulpicius Severus, *Life of Martin* 10.1–3, 106.

37. Sulpicius Severus, *Life of Martin* 10.2–3, 106.

Sulpicius goes on to state that: "[The] place was so hidden and remote that it might not require the solitude of the wilderness. For, from the one side it was encircled by the precipitous cliff of a high mountain; the river Loire had closed the remaining plain a little bit with its receding bay . . ."[38] It is reasonable to assume that Martin's secluded locale was intended for much more than rest from apostolic labors and the pressures of episcopal administration. The monastic bishop's retreat from crowds posing a distraction to the spiritual life is akin to that of the desert fathers, Arsenius and Sisoes, thus further testifying to the early transmission of the Eastern ascetic ideal.[39] Similarities between Sulpicius' description of Martin's monastery—later titled Marmoutier on the basis of the Latin appellation, *Maius monasterium*—and a typical Eastern lavra have in fact been noted by scholars.[40] I therefore posit that the saint deliberately chose Marmoutier (and, earlier, Gallinara) for the purpose of natural contemplation, that is, the genuine perception of created beings in relation to God and each other, the attempt of the rational mind, the spiritual intellect, and the senses to discern the divine presence, will, and glory in the material world.[41]

On a related note, Sulpicius has depicted Martin as an imitator of our Lord Jesus, who went up a mountain to pray after ministering to the multitudes in Galilee (Matt 14:23; Mark 1:35; Luke 5:16). He has therefore tacitly suggested that a certain degree of peace and solitude are required for genuine contemplation. It is evident that Sulpicius maintained that practical asceticism and contemplation led to true theology as understood by the Byzantines: an undefinable relationship with God, who is above all knowledge. This is in contradistinction to the mere syllogisms formulated by most contemporary academics, including yours truly.[42] According to Sulpicius, it is precisely this mysterious association which enabled Martin to perform his many Christ-like feats, whatever his vocation happened to be at the time. I must emphasize that the holy ascetic's commitment to, and resulting participation in, the Lord is evidenced by a wide range of miracles within the *Martiniana*, including striking exorcisms and deeply

38. Sulpicius Severus, *Life of Martin* 10.4, 106.

39. *Apophthegmata Patrum* (*Collectio Graeca alphabetica*) (PG 65, 98D–100C, 401A–B); Bosivert, "Origins," 961–62.

40. Lawrence, *Medieval Monasticism*, 11–12; James, "Archaeology and the Merovingian Monastery," 36; Peebles, *Sulpicius Severus*, 117 n. 2.

41. Paffhausen, "Natural Contemplation in St. Maximus the Confessor and St. Isaac the Syrian," 48.

42. Nichols, *Byzantine Gospel*, 193.

moving resurrections. We shall limit our discussion to those signifying his restoration of the condition of creation before the ancestral fall.

Sulpicius' letter to his mother-in-law, Bassula, is known for its moving account of Martin's repose and burial.[43] His description of the holy bishop's final journey is highly relevant to our analysis.[44] The hagiographer relates how Martin ventured with his disciples to a certain parish at Candice (in what is now central France) to restore peace amongst its clergy, having also foreseen his repose at this location. On the way, the bishop spotted certain birds diving into the River Loire, catching fish. Martin likened the ravenous birds to demons, which similarly ambush and capture unwary prey. He subsequently commanded the birds to leave the fish alone and depart to a dry and deserted land (i.e., a place typically associated with evil in hagiographical literature).[45] Sulpicius affirms that Martin "used that command with which he was accustomed to drive out the demons."[46] The scattered birds immediately formed a flock and departed, causing Martin's disciples to marvel at his power.

Sulpicius' general audience no doubt interpreted Martin's rebuke of the birds as just punishment for their demon-like gluttony. However, the audiences of Late Antiquity and the Middle Ages would have also appreciated Sulpicius' simultaneous depiction of Martin as a master of the sensible/material and intelligible/immaterial realms as represented by the birds and demons, respectively.[47] Furthermore, the sense of wonder that

---

43. Burton, "Introduction" to *Sulpicius Severus' Vita Martini*, 5; Peebles, "Introduction" to *Sulpicius Severus*, 87; Goodrich, "Introduction" to *Sulpicius Severus*, 13; Mertens, *Old English Lives of St Martin of Tours*, 26–27. Taken at face value, this letter appears to have been published without the author's consent. Sulpicius asks Bassula within the opening paragraph not to read it to anyone, playfully charging her with intercepting and disseminating writings that he has intended for others (Sulpicius Severus, *Letter to Bassula* 1–5, 334–36). However, given the letter's significant subject matter it is highly likely that he intended it to reach a wider audience. Sulpicius has expressed similar reluctance with respect to the publication of his *Life of Martin*, partly to the subvert the prevailing Greco-Roman literary values.

44. Sulpicius Severus, *Letter to Bassula* 6–16, esp. 7–8, 336–42.

45. Sulpicius Severus, *Letter to Bassula* 8, 338.

46. "Then, with a powerful expression he ordered that they should make for dry and deserted regions, abandoning that eddy on which they were floating; evidently, among those birds he used that command with which he was accustomed to drive out the demons." Sulpicius Severus, *Letter to Bassula* 8, 338.

47. For a thorough exploration of the Christian education offered in Late Antique Gaul, see, Haarhoff, *Schools of Gaul*, 180–87. As concerns the continuation of the Latin rhetorical curriculum within the region, see Mathisen, "Bishops, Barbarians, and the

Sulpicius attributes to Martin's companions deliberately echoes the Twelve Disciples' reaction to Christ's rebuke of the winds (Matt 8:23–27; Mark 4:35–41; Luke 8:22–25). Sulpicius has thus presented Martin as capable of inspiring the same wonder as God the Son by virtue of his imitation of (and resulting participation in) him.

In the *Dialogues* 2.9, the hagiographer, citing Gallus, relates how Martin encountered a heifer afflicted by a demon as he once returned home from Trèves.[48] According to Sulpicius, the animal posed an immediate danger to the people living nearby, and "had already harmfully pierced many." The monastic bishop, "after raising his hand, ordered the hostile beast to stand still[,]" then rebuked the fallen angel that he alone could see riding on its back.[49] The ascetic displayed compassion for the animal, which he perceived as naturally "innocent" (*innoxium*).[50] As to be expected, both the cow and the demon instantly obeyed the bishop.[51] Sulpicius accordingly hints once more at Martin's fulfilment of Adam's role as a God-appointed arbiter of the sensible and intelligible realms, here typified by the animal and a being which was formerly part of the cosmic harmony as an angel. Interestingly, the cow is described as having prostrated itself before the saint, who then instructs it to rejoin its herd. The story thus echoes Christ's compassionate dismissal of the Gerasene demoniac (Mark 5:1–20; Luke 8:26–39) whilst at the same time demonstrating Sulpicius' conviction that Martin's spiritual feats stemmed from his cooperation with God (as established through practical asceticism and contemplation, rather than any innate power).

At the end of the chapter, Sulpicius, again referring to Gallus, describes Martin's encounter with certain hunters during a tour of the parishes in Gaul. According to the bishop's disciple, Martin chanced upon the hunters' dogs in pursuit of a hare. Pitying the latter's desperate attempt to escape death, he ordered the canines to cease. The narrator emphasizes the animals' sudden stop, as though they had been chained or rooted in their

---

'Dark Ages,'" 3–19.

48. "When Martin was returning from Trèves, a cow was made hostile which a demon was tormenting." Sulpicius Severus, *Dialogues* 2.9.1, 258.

49. "That [animal], after abandoning its herd, was being led into people and, butting with its head, had already harmfully pierced many. Martin, after raising his hand, ordered the hostile beast to stand still." Sulpicius Severus, *Dialogues* 2.9.1–2, 258.

50. "'Depart, o calamitous one, from the beast,' he said, 'and cease to torment an innocent animal.'" Sulpicius Severus, *Dialogues* 2.9.3, 258.

51. Sulpicius Severus, *Dialogues* 2.9.4, 258.

tracks.[52] This story is somewhat unusual in hagiographical literature, since the rescued animal is allowed to remain wild and free without rendering any service to the saint.[53] Yet this supposed peculiarity stems from Sulpicius' desire to underscore the bishop's Christ-like care of all creatures, even those which may be considered minor.

In the *Dialogues* 2.3, Sulpicius describes how Martin was attacked by certain imperial officials during another tour of the Gallic churches.[54] More to the point, the bishop happened to startle the mules guiding their vehicle as he proceeded beyond them, thereby causing the animals to rush sidewards and tangle their traces. This incident revealed the true character of the officials, who savagely beat Martin for delaying their journey, finally rendering him unconscious before returning to their vehicle. The mules, however, refused to move, remaining "fixed in the earth, [. . .] as if they were bronze statues."[55] Unsurprisingly, the officials turned their anger to the animals, repeatedly whipping them to urge them forward. Eventually, the officials discovered from passersby that the traveler whom they had abused was none other than Martin, renowned for his holiness. Consequently, they set out on foot in search of the bishop who had since been revived by his disciples and was continuing his journey. When they eventually caught up to Martin they genuinely pleaded for his forgiveness, begging to be released. Sulpicius relates that Martin displayed his characteristic altruism and the gift of foresight before restoring the officials' control over the mules.

Two further aspects of this story are of interest to us. Firstly, it is suggested that the mules were startled at the sight of the holy ascetic; their haste in moving aside is not meant to be attributed to their wild nature but their awe in the presence of Martin. Indeed, the mules' fidelity to God—evidenced by their patient endurance of violence, identical to that of the monastic bishop—is tacitly contrasted with the officials' frustration, savage conduct, and "stupid heads" (*bruta pectora*). Secondly, the saint himself does not forbid the mules from assisting the officials. Rather, the animals are held back "by a divine will" (*diuino numine*).[56] More precisely, it is suggested that

52. Sulpicius Severus, *Dialogues* 2.9.6, 260.

53. Alexander, *Saints and Animals in the Middle Ages*, 3, 16, 39, 118, 128.

54. Sulpicius Severus, *Dialogues* 2.3.1–10, 226–30.

55. "When all those [mules], fixed in the earth, had stiffened as if they were bronze statues—when the drivers more deeply brought forth a cry, and their whips resounded from different directions—through and through, they were not set in motion at all." Sulpicius Severus, *Dialogues* 2.3.6, 228.

56. "The miserable men did not know what they might do, nor could they now

God displayed his anger with the officials by restraining creatures which ultimately belonged to him. In fact, Sulpicius, reiterating Gallus, affirms that the officials recognized that the earth itself could have reacted against their abuse of Martin by swallowing them alive.[57] This assertion likewise attests to Martin's role as a Christ-like ruler of creation.

In the *Dialogues* 3.9.4, Sulpicius relates how, during another journey, Gallus and a presbyter named Refrigerius witnessed Martin ordering an "wicked beast" (*mala bestia*), that is, a serpent, to reverse its course as it swam across a river towards them.[58] Interestingly, Sulpicius recalls Gallus' affirmation that Martin sighed at the fact that whilst such creatures heard him, most people did not.[59] This story functions as a tacit criticism of those who do not obey Martin's teachings, which, I must add, were taken to ultimately proceed from Christ.[60]

Let us on move on to the final story by Sulpicius attesting to Martin's role as Christ's co-worker in the preservation and renewal of the created order. In the *Dialogues* 3.10.1–4 the hagiographer summarizes Gallus' account of a miraculous catch of fish at Martin's exhortation during a certain Paschal cycle.[61] According to Sulpicius, the monastic bishop once requested to eat a pike during this sacred season, as was his custom. Cato the deacon (who served as the administrator of Martin's monastery and was responsible for fishing) replied that neither he nor the local merchants had been able to catch any from the nearby river. The holy ascetic nevertheless instructed the deacon to cast his net, their fellow monks looking on with every hope of success. Sulpicius in turn affirms that Cato immediately caught a huge pike. Interestingly, Sulpicius has borrowed language

---

further ignore that, however much with their dull minds, they should acknowledge that they themselves were being restrained by a divine will." Sulpicius Severus, *Dialogues* 2.3.7, 228.

57. Sulpicius Severus, *Dialogues* 2.3.9, 230.

58. "A serpent cutting across the river towards the bank, on which we had stopped, began to swim near: 'In the name of the Lord,' said he [i.e., Martin], 'I order you to turn back.' Thereupon, the wicked beast cast itself back at the word of the saint and, before our eyes, went over to a more distant bank. When we all perceived that (not without wonder), he [i.e., Martin], uttering a sigh more deeply, affirmed: 'The serpents listen to me, and men do not listen!'" Sulpicius Severus, *Dialogues* 3.9.4, 322–24.

59. This lament is echoed by Postumanius within the *Dialogues* 1.14.8, 160.

60. Alexander, *Saints and Animals in the Middle Ages*, 36.

61. Sulpicius Severus, *Dialogues* 3.10.1–4, 324–26.

from Statius' *Thebaid* in his reiteration of Gallus' story.[62] Notwithstanding the stylistic influence of the Latin classics, this account closely resembles Peter's miraculous draughts of fish at Christ's call, both before and after the resurrection (Luke 5:1–11; John 21:1–14). Indeed, Gallus, as presented by Sulpicius, eventually affirms with respect to Martin that: "Truly, this disciple of Christ—a zealous imitator of the virtues borne by the Savior, which He set forth as an example to His saints—showed Christ working in himself; Who, always glorifying His saint, bestowed onto the single person gifts of different [spiritual] charisms."[63]

In summary, Sulpicius has consistently depicted Martin as a compassionate lord of the natural and inhabited worlds on account of his imitation of Christ, Antony, and other Eastern monks. The author continues to challenge his audiences to attain Martin's level of faith and commitment to the gospel. We are in fact called by Suplicius to participate in the redemption of the universe as initiated by our Lord and Savior through his incarnation, passion, and resurrection, and carried on by his saints through their similar perfect conduct, whatever their respective contexts. As indicated above, this requires a certain method according to Sulpicius, namely, progression through practical asceticism, contemplation, and the resulting communion with God, regarded as a constant, iterative process. This experience certainly is not limited to monks and nuns, hence Sulpicius' publication of the *Martiniana* for all of Christendom.

The influence of the *Martiniana* in the history of hagiographical literature can hardly be underestimated. Sulpicius' writings were disseminated by Bassula, Paulinus, and St. Niceta of Remesiana, amongst others. The life subsequently served as a model for numerous Latin hagiographies throughout Late Antiquity and the Middle Ages, beginning with that on St. Ambrose of Milan commissioned by St. Augustine of Hippo. It exerted special influence on St. Adomnán of Iona's magnificent *Life of St. Columba*.[64] The work eventually reached Byzantium, as evidenced by its summation on the part of the fifth-century historian, Sozomen.[65] The *Dialogues*, too, enjoyed great renown, undoubtedly inspiring St. Gregory the Great to compose a similar work on the numerous ascetics of Italy. Most importantly, the example of Martin led to countless more saints of similar stature in the

---

62. Peebles, *Sulpicius Severus*, 238 n.2.

63. Sulpicius Severus, *Dialogues* 3.10.5, 326.

64. Peebles, "Introduction" to *Sulpicius Severus*, 92–96, esp. 92–93.

65. Sozomen, Ἐκκλησιαστικὴ ἱστορία 3.14.38–41, 134–38.

Latin West, his legacy being comparable to that of Antony in this regard. In fact, Sulpicius states in a letter to a deacon named Aurelius that Martin, had he been given the opportunity, would have born witness to Christ to the point of death just like the apostles and many others amongst the faithful during the reigns of Nero and Decius. However, it was his destiny to endure a bloodless martyrdom, specifically through his ascetical and pastoral labors.[66] In fact, as Sulpicius makes clear from his wider literary corpus, Martin, like Antony, was not simply a witness to Christ; our Lord made himself known in the person of the saint, thus inspiring countless generations of our Western forebears to follow him.

On a final note, let us reflect on the fact that the Orthodox Christian experience was common to the Greek East and Latin West throughout the first millennium, extending from the deserts of Egypt, Mesopotamia, and Asia Minor through the woods of the continent to the Irish bogs and English Marshlands. This was a tremendous feat on the part of countless men and women from amongst the clergy and laity, especially if we bear in mind the constant danger posed by natural disasters, untreatable illnesses, and malevolent human forces, including heretics, barbarians, and bandits, to those who dared to travel during this time. Moreover, we have a loving intercessor before the Lord, our holy father Martin of Tours, who will no doubt assist us in attaining his abounding humility, ascetical fortitude, and compassion for the entire creation if we but pray to him. This was certainly the intention of the incredibly influential and eloquent hagiographer, Sulpicius Severus, in composing the *Martiniana*. Let us show him the honor in reading, and taking to heart, his works.

---

66. Sulpicius Severus, *Letter to Aurelius the Deacon* 8–14, 328–33.

9

The Saints of Early Ireland and Britain

I pray You, noble Jesu, that as You have graciously granted me joyfully to imbibe the words of Your knowledge, so You will also of Your bounty grant me to come at length to Yourself, the Fount of all wisdom, and to dwell in Your presence for ever.—St. Bede the Venerable, *A History of the English Church and People* 5.24[1]

THE FIRST EVIDENCE FOR the presence of the church in Britain dates from the third century, when the Orthodox Christian faith was introduced by Roman imperial administrators and soldiers to the native British elite who had surrendered to the Continental superpower during the reign of the emperor Claudius.[2] It is significant that the Romano-British faithful were subjected to sporadic persecution under the pagan imperial authorities just like the remainder of the church, as evidenced by the martyrdoms of Sts. Aaron, Julius, and Alban in the mid-third century, later recorded by St. Bede the Venerable and his major historical influence, St. Gildas the Wise.[3] Culturally, the church transmitted written law to Britain via the Latin language, in addition to classical and patristic literature. As concerns the structure of the early British Church, the first dioceses were based on Roman civil structures. Subsequently, bishops from London, York, and

---

1. Bede the Venerable, *History of the English Church and People* 5.4, 331.

2. Bede the Venerable, *History of the English Church and People* 1.2–3, 40–42; Dunn, *Emergence of Monasticism*, 138; Davies, "Introduction" to *Celtic Spirituality*, 20.

3. Bede the Venerable, *History of the English Church and People* 1.6–7, 43–47; Gildas the Wise, *Ruin of Britain* 10, 24–27.

Lincoln/Colchester attended the Council of Arles in c. 314, which was intended to remedy the division caused by hardhearted heretics known as the Donatists, and which served as a prototype for the first Ecumenical Council convened by St. Constantine the Great.[4] The Romano-British Church gradually contracted after the withdrawal of the imperial forces in 409, and the subsequent Irish, Pictish, and Germanic invasions. By the fifth century, it became limited to the areas of modern-day Scotland and Northern England, specifically Strathclyde and Cumbria, in addition to Wales, Devon, and Cornwall.[5] An important source for this period is Gildas' hortatory treatise *On the Ruin of Britain*. In short, the church father recorded the history of his people as a means of censuring their vices and turning them back to the Lord, thereby resembling the prophets of the Old Testament whilst at the same time anticipating charismatic figures of Byzantium like St. Symeon the New Theologian.

The British Church went on to influence Ireland through trade and migration, and it is likely that the faithful from its Western region helped establish the first Christian community on the Emerald Isle during the fifth century.[6] Palladius, a deacon from Auxerre in Gaul, was soon commissioned by St. Celestine of Rome to shepherd the early Irish and combat a heresy stemming from a cleric named Pelagius, who was possibly a native of Wales originally named Morgan.[7] In short, Pelagius argued that a person can attain salvation entirely through their own efforts, thereby contradicting the testimony of St. Paul the Apostle with respect to the importance of divine grace in our spiritual development.[8] Palladius was ordained the first bishop of Ireland, working primarily in its south-east territory where he also established the first Celtic monasteries.[9] He was followed by one of the most celebrated saints in history, namely, Patrick the Enlightener and Equal-to-the-Apostles, who was directly inspired by God to convert the Irish of the north, especially within the regions of Ulster and Connacht. Christians from Gaul likely aided Patrick in his evangelic work,

---

4. Dunn, *Emergence of Monasticism*, 139; Davies, "Introduction" to *Celtic Spirituality*, 20.

5. Davies, "Introduction" to *Celtic Spirituality*, 21–22.

6. Dunn, *Emergence of Monasticism*, 142; Davies, "Introduction" to *Celtic Spirituality*, 16.

7. Dunn, *Emergence of Monasticism*, 142–43; Davies, "Introduction" to *Celtic Spirituality*, 16; Meek, *Quest for Celtic Christianity*, 128–37.

8. Holmes, "Preface to Volume I. of the Edinburgh Edition" of *Augustin*, 3.

9. Dunn, *Emergence of Monasticism*, 142.

and it is noteworthy that the positive relationship between the missionary and monastic networks of Ireland and the Continent continued for several centuries.[10] Patrick was from a Christian family from northwest Britain, somewhere around Carlisle. His father was a deacon, his grandfather was a presbyter, yet he himself did not surrender to Christ until he was captured by pirates and taken to Ireland as a boy. In captivity, he spent his days tending sheep in constant prayer in direct conversation with God, thus foreshadowing the hesychasts of Byzantium. Although he managed to escape slavery with the assistance of Divine Providence, he was compelled to return to Ireland as an adult after having been ordained, primarily on account of a vision from God.[11] Patrick has described his outstanding apostolic enterprise in his written *Confession/Testament*, which serves as a strategic reply to his jealous critics, a formal declaration of his adherence to the central tenets of the faith (such as the doctrine of the Holy Trinity), and a wondrous means of preaching the gospel, by movingly attesting to God's active presence within his life.[12]

A synod was eventually held in Ireland in the late sixth century. This was later attributed to Patrick, attesting to his immense popularity as the island's patron saint. The canons produced by the gathering indicate that the church in Ireland was initially governed by bishops in dioceses based on the territories of the indigenous tribes.[13] Around this time, numerous monasteries and lay communities were established throughout the Emerald Isle by the beloved miracle worker, St. Brigit of Kildare, who was also admired for her wisdom and compassion.[14] This was in addition to St. Finnian of Clonard and his disciples, traditionally referred to as the "Twelve Apostles of Ireland."[15] Amongst these disciples were Sts. Columba of Iona and Brendan of Clonfert, otherwise known as the Navigator. The latter is the subject of a fascinating text titled *The Voyage of Brendan*, a Christian equivalent to Homer's *Odyssey* and Virgil's *Aeneid* that went on to influence

---

10. Dunn, *Emergence of Monasticism*, 143–44; Davies, "Introduction" to *Celtic Spirituality*, 16–17.

11. Patrick of Ireland, *Patrick's Declaration of the Great Works of God* 1–25, esp. 23–27, 67–73.

12. O'Loughlin, "Patrick Tradition" in "Introduction" to *Celtic Spirituality*, 28–29.

13. Davies, "Introduction" to *Celtic Spirituality*, 17.

14. *Life of St. Brigit the Virgin by Cogitosus* and *Irish Life of Brigit*, in *Celtic Spirituality*, 122–54.

15. Woods, "Ireland," 658.

the renowned fantasy author, J. R. R. Tolkien.[16] By the seventh century, the territorial dioceses of Ireland were partly superseded by monastic networks known as *paruchiae*, so that abbots had significant authority within society. In fact, bishops worked largely from monasteries whilst willingly submitting themselves to their respective abbots for the purpose of retaining their humility.[17] Yet the ecclesiastical structure of Ireland was eventually made more consistent with that of Western Europe in the eleventh and twelfth centuries through the influence of monastic reforms originating from Burgundy, in addition to the conquests of the Anglo-Normans.[18]

Columba, of royal descent, began his apostolic vocation by founding monasteries in the regions of Derry and Durrow. He was eventually compelled to leave his native home in 563, either to avoid dynastic politics or repent his involvement in what has been described as the first world's copyright dispute, one which inspired his kin to take arms against the reigning high king.[19] Whatever the case may be, through his ascetic life in exile, Columba became a wonderworker and even greater missionary, founding a monastic community off the Scottish coast at the isle of Iona, from where he set out with his disciples to convert the Picts.[20] The Orthodox faith thus came to dominate the Western part of Scotland through the Latin and Irish languages, with Iona eventually becoming the head of a large network of highly learned Christian communities that extended to central Ireland, East Anglia, and Northumbria.[21] These communities produced some of the most wonderful manuscripts in history, such as the illustrious *Book of Kells*.[22] The life of Columba—who wondrously shepherded his Irish and Pictish flocks as a prophet, miracle worker, converser with angels, and experiencer of the divine light—has been eloquently recorded by his relative and monastic successor, St. Adomnán. The latter

---

16. *Voyage of Brendan* in *Celtic Spirituality*, 155–90; Davies, "Introduction" to *Celtic Spirituality*, 34. For a complete collection of the medieval works on the ascetic and missionary, including a modern commentary, see *Brendaniana: St. Brendan the Voyager in Story and Legend*.

17. Dunn, *Emergence of Monasticism*, 147–48; Davies, "Introduction" to *Celtic Spirituality*, 17–18.

18. Davies, "Introduction" to *Celtic Spirituality*, 20.

19. Sharpe, "Introduction" to Adomnán of Iona, *Life of St. Columba*.

20. Bede the Venerable, *History of the English Church and People* 3.3–4, 141–45; Sharpe, "Introduction" to Adomnán of Iona, *Life of St. Columba*.

21. Davies, "Introduction" to *Celtic Spirituality*, 18.

22. See, for example, *Book of Kells* (complete details within the bibliography).

happens to be one of the most significant authors of ecclesiastical canons and state legislation, having promulgated the famed "Law of Innocents" (*Lex innocentium*), which defended the rights of women, children, and clerics during times of conflict.[23]

By the sixth century, most of Britain had come under the control of pagan Anglo-Saxons. The incredibly influential bishop of Rome, St. Gregory the Great, therefore established a mission to Kent, entrusting it to an Italian Benedictine monk by the name of Augustine who eventually became the first bishop of Canterbury.[24] With the assistance of St. Bertha, the Frankish wife of King Aethelberht of Kent, St. Augustine of Canterbury had considerable success. Gregory therefore announced Augustine's baptism of more than ten thousand people on a single Christmas day in a letter to Bishop Eulogius of Alexandria in July of 598.[25] Augustine's mission temporarily lost ground during the period in which Eadbald, Aethelberht's successor, reverted to paganism. Nonetheless, Augustine had an enduring legacy, having founded Christ Church Cathedral and the monastery of Sts. Peter and Paul in Canterbury, in addition to the episcopal sees of London and Rochester. To be sure, numerous other monasteries were soon established in these locations. Meanwhile, outside of Kent, bishops were appointed to individual kingdoms, thereby creating vast dioceses.[26] St. Theodore of Tarsus—a Greek contemporary of St. Maximus the Confessor and fellow defender of Christ's two wills (i.e., the human and the divine)—was sent to Canterbury by St. Agatho of Rome in 669, from where he established more conventional dioceses throughout England.[27] Furthermore, Theodore was tasked with convincing the Celtic Christians to forsake an obsolete method for the dating of Easter and adopt that used by the wider church, principally for the sake of spiritual unity. He successfully accomplished this at the Synod of Whitby in 664, which marks the fusion between the Celtic and Anglo-Saxon Christian

---

23. Bede the Venerable, *History of the English Church and People* 5.15, 293–95; Marsden, "Prologue" to *Illustrated Life of Columba*, 11–28; Wooding et al., *Adomnán of Iona: Theologian, Lawmaker, Peacemaker*.

24. Gregory the Great, *Registrum epistolarum* 6.51 and 59 (PL 77, 836A–B, 842C–843B); Bede the Venerable, *History of the English Church and People* 1.23–33, 66–91; Ricci, "Gregory's Missions to the Barbarians," 47–55.

25. *Registrum epistolarum* 8.30 (PL 77, 931C–934A).

26. Dunn, *Emergence of Monasticism*, 195.

27. For a summary of the church father's life and activity in Edessa, Constantinople, Rome, and Canterbury, see Siemens, *Christology of Theodore of Tarsus*, 1–20.

communities.[28] Hence, this unique aspect of the church of the first millennium is now commonly referred to as "Insular" in the positive sense, that is, as pertaining to the British Isles. In addition, it is worth mentioning that Theodore established scholarly rigor within the Insular clerical ranks, to which he bestowed many writings of the Byzantine fathers.

The Gregorian mission initially enjoyed greater success in the north, especially since King Edwin of Northumbria married the Christian princess Ethelberga, daughter of Bertha and Aethelberht. St. Paulinus, a Roman monk sent to England by Gregory and the first bishop of York who had labored tirelessly in Kent, accompanied Ethelberga to Northumbria, where he baptized the king.[29] Sadly, St. Edwin was eventually defeated by a tyrannical rival, so that his immediate successors split his kingdom and reverted to the old religion. The Christian faith therefore declined in Northumbria until the accession of the Bernician prince, St. Oswald, who was highly praised by Bede owing to his piety. Oswald reunited the kingdom and turned to Columba to provide him with a bishop. Whilst the first candidate proved unsuitable, the second, St. Aidan, was instrumental in restoring Christianity within Northumbria. Aidan founded a monastic center off the Northumbrian coast at Lindisfarne, where he combined evangelistic and pastoral activities with a contemplative ascetic life, likewise to the admiration of Bede.[30]

At Lindisfarne, Aidan likely preached to a key figure in the Insular history of our church, namely, St. Cuthbert the Wonderworker.[31] Cuthbert was called to experience holiness at a young age after a brief career as a soldier, eventually becoming an ascetic paragon and beloved patron of the poor and animals. On entering the Holy Monastery of Melrose, also constructed by Aidan, he became the spiritual son of its prior (i.e., the second

28. The influential historian of Insular Christianity, Thomas O'Loughlin, rightly contended that the Celtic patristic and hagiographical authors considered themselves part of the broader Latin ecclesial framework and would have been scandalised by the notion of a distinct "Celtic Church." O'Loughlin, *Celtic Theology*, 10, 14, 17–18. See also, Stancliffe, "Irish Tradition in Northumbria After the Synod of Whitby," 19–42.

29. Bede the Venerable, *History of the English Church and People* 2.9, 14, 16–17 and 20, 112–15, 126–27, 129–31, 135–36.

30. For more on Sts. Oswald and Aidan, see Bede the Venerable, *History of the English Church and People* 3.1–3 and 3.5–6, 138–42, 145–48; Colgrave, "Introduction" to *Two Lives of Saint Cuthbert*, 5–6; Dunn, *Emergence of Monasticism*, 195–96.

31. Colgrave, "Introduction" to *Two Lives of Saint Cuthbert*, 6.

in charge after the abbot), St. Boisil.[32] The Venerable Bede has revealed that Boisil acquired the gifts of discernment and foresight from the Holy Spirit, at one time revealing to Cuthbert the entire course of the young monk's virtuous life.[33] It is relevant to our current experience that there was an outbreak of plague during this period; the contagious bacterial disease was quite common throughout the Middle Ages, usually consisting in fever and delirium in addition to the formation of buboes and severe infection of the lungs. Sts. Boisil and Cuthbert both contracted the illness, the former finally reposing in the Lord on account of it, yet—it must be emphasized—still retaining his characteristic spirit of joy.[34] The latter recovered and went on to perform numerous prophecies, healings, and exorcisms as a prior, missionary, hermit, and bishop, even recalling to life a dying youth during a tour of the outer villages of his diocese. Indeed, he gained the ability to heal those who had the plague by God's grace, a major instance of which has been described by Bede as follows.

> At the same time there suddenly arose in those parts a most grievous pestilence, and brought with it destruction so severe that in some large villages and estates once crowded with inhabitants, only a small and scattered remnant, and sometimes none at all, remained. So the most holy father Cuthbert, diligently traversing his diocese, did not cease to bring the ministry of the word and the help of much-needed consolation to the poor few who remained. Coming to one village and having helped by his exhortations all whom he found, he said to his priest: "Do you think that anyone is left in these parts who needs to be visited and exhorted by us; or have we seen all who are in trouble and can we now pass on to others?" The priest, looking round everywhere, saw a woman standing at a distance who, having lost one son a little while before, was now holding his brother in her arms at the point of death; her eyes, streaming with tears, bore witness both to her past and her present troubles. The priest pointed her out to the man of God, who did not delay but, approaching her and giving her his blessing, kissed the boy and said to the mother: "Do not fear nor be sad; for your infant will be healed

---

32. *Vita Sancti Cuthberti Auctore Anonymo* [i.e., *Anonymous Life of St. Cuthbert*] 1.3–7, 2.3–5, 3.5, and 4.2–7, 64–73, 78–87, 100–3, 112–23; *Vita Sancti Cuthberti Auctore Beda* [i.e., *Life of St. Cuthbert*] 1–5, 10, 12, 20, 25–26, and 29–33, 188–91, 194–97, 222–25, 238–43, 252–61.

33. Bede the Venerable, *Life of St. Cuthbert* 6, 172–75.

34. Bede the Venerable, *Life of St. Cuthbert* 8, 180–85.

and will live, nor will anyone else be missing from your home through this plague." The mother herself and her son lived long afterwards to bear testimony to the truth of this prophecy.[35]

It is significant that that this wonderful saint, whom we affectionately hail as "Wonderworker," eventually contracted a debilitating illness, one so severe that it greatly prevented it him from moving his body for the three weeks leading up to his repose, which he foresaw and courageously prepared for through prayer.[36] Bede, citing a witness named Herefrith, affirms that God also cut him off from his flock for five days at this point, in which he was assaulted by the enemy, alone. The church father reveals that God's purpose in testing Cuthbert was to completely purify him and demonstrate to his adversaries that nothing could prevail against his faith. The holy ascetic thus serves as an example to us in this period of trial and temptation seeing that he never asked to be freed from his affliction, trusting instead in God's mercy and love whilst prioritizing the needs of others. His compassion and altruism are evidenced by the fact that he healed a disciple from chronic dysentery during his final days in the flesh with a mere touch. Moreover, he took the opportunity to educate and comfort his disciples, as well as return all the gifts that he had received from his friends. And so, on the 20th of March 687, after receiving Holy Communion from Herefrith, he gave up his soul to the Lord while praising him for all things.

Likely from a wealthy family, Bede was sent by his parents at the age of seven to be raised and educated by St. Benedict Biscop at the monastery which the latter had founded at Wearmouth in Northumbria.[37] Benedict had been on many pilgrimages throughout the Continent and endowed his monastery with various writings of the fathers, consequently establishing one of the greatest libraries in the West during the Middle Ages.[38] Whilst we only have scant information from Bede regarding his own formation and monastic tonsure, we can assume that he eagerly embraced the ascetic life owing to his later emphasis on the importance of discipline

---

35. Bede the Venerable, *Life of St. Cuthbert* 33, 258–61.

36. *Anonymous Life of St. Cuthbert* 4.11–13, 128–31; Bede the Venerable, *Life of St. Cuthbert* 34 and 37–39, 260–61, 270–85.

37. Bede the Venerable, *History of the English Church and People* 5.24, 328–31; Brown, "Bede's Life in Context," 5–6.

38. For more on the great monastic founder and patron, see Bede the Venerable, *Lives of the Abbots of Wearmouth and Jarrow* 1–14. Concerning the libraries at Wearmouth and Jarrow, see Love, "World of Latin Learning," 43–46.

and obedience, as well as his clear love of knowledge.[39] On becoming a monk, Bede devoted himself to study of the Scriptures, observing something akin to the popular Western monastic rule formulated by St. Benedict of Nursia. He later moved with his warden and the former assistant of Benedict Biscop, St. Ceolfrith, to a new community at nearby Jarrow. He worked diligently between Wearmouth and Jarrow, approximately eleven kilometers apart, before he was ordained a deacon at the age of nineteen and presbyter when thirty.[40] Like Cuthbert, he was once forced to endure pestilence and famine because of the plague. Interestingly, the written *Life of Ceolfrith* mentions that only one small boy—most likely Bede—remained fit enough to chant at Jarrow for some time.[41] Besides laboring in the scriptorium as a copyist and original author, he spent his life with his brethren in regular performance of the Divine Office, which included recitation of the psalms and corporate prayers in addition to biblical readings. Moreover, he undertook arduous manual work to cultivate humility and master his emotions and impulses.[42]

Unknown to most people, Bede was far more than a chronicler of the church, having composed numerous lives of saints, multiple commentaries on the Scriptures, and even treatises on grammar and the philosophy of time.[43] He had masterful knowledge of the classical authors and, more importantly, the Byzantine and Continental fathers of the church, being an expert in Latin rhetoric with some skill in the Hellenic tongue. His native language was Old English, specifically the dialect spoken in Northumbria. It is quite striking that this key figure in the history of the church—and one of the most celebrated minds of the medieval world—did not advance to the rank of bishop or travel abroad, preferring to live humbly in poverty at the Holy Monastery of Sts. Peter and Paul encompassing Wearmouth and Jarrow. In fact, he has hardly mentioned himself with his vast written corpus, and we are indebted to a disciple named Cuthbert for a record of his final moments in the flesh in 735. In short, about two weeks before Pascha, Bede became ill and had trouble breathing. He remained cheerful despite

39. Brown, "Bede's Life in Context," 5–6.

40. Bede the Venerable, *History of the English Church and People* 5.24, 328–29; Brown, "Bede's Life in Context," 6–7.

41. *Anonymous History of Abbot Ceolfrith* 14; Brown, "Bede's Life in Context," 8.

42. Brown, "Bede's Life in Context," 7–9.

43. For the church father's complete bibliography, see "Notes on Editions and Translations," in *Cambridge Companion to Bede*, xii–xiii.

his weakness, continuing to teach his students and chant the psalms whilst remembering the positive attitude of the fathers towards death. Imitating Cuthbert the Wonderworker, he also distributed whatever gifts that he had received throughout his life to his fellow monks.[44] During this time, Bede hoped to finish compiling extracts from the writings of St. Isidore of Seville, as well as an Anglo-Saxon translation of the gospel of St. John the Theologian. On the eve of the feast of the Ascension, aware that the hour of his repose was near, he exhorted his disciples to record his dictation of the gospel's final chapters. Unable to accompany his brethren during a procession of holy relics, Bede was left with a young scribe named Wilbert. According to the relevant primary source, the church father declared:

> "If it be the will of my Maker, the time has come when I shall be freed from the body and return to Him Who created me out of nothing when I had no being. I have had a long life, and the merciful Judge has ordered it graciously. The time of my departure is at hand, and my soul longs to see Christ my King in His beauty." […] Then the same lad, named Wilbert, said again, "Dear master, there is still one sentence still unfinished." "Very well," he replied, "write it down." After a short while the lad said, "Now it is finished." "You have spoken truly," he replied: "It is well finished. Now raise my head in your hands, for it would give me great joy to sit facing the holy place where I used to pray, so that I may sit and call on my Father." And thus, on the floor of his cell, he chanted, "Glory be to Father, and to the Son, and to the Holy Spirit" to its ending, and breathed his last.[45]

By the late seventh century, owing to the efforts of the church fathers described above, most of England had embraced the Orthodox faith. Remarkably, the faithful of rival kingdoms in Britain and Ireland acknowledged each other's saints. This is demonstrated by King Ælfwald of East Anglia, who commissioned the *Life of St. Guthlac* even though its subject came from Mercia. It has been posited that the saint was of interest to the ruler since he had established his hermitage in the borderland known as Crowland. Furthermore, the favorable portrayal of King Æthelbald of Mercia in the life suggests that relations between the two realms were positive at the time.[46] Judging from the wider hagiographical tradition, it is, in fact,

---

44. *Letter of Cuthbert to Cuthwin*, 18–20.

45. *Letter of Cuthbert to Cuthwin*, 20.

46. Felix, *Vita Sancti Guthlaci* [i.e., *Life of St. Guthlac*] 40, 49, and 51, 124–27, 148–51, 160–63. For a summary of the Mercian king's life, see Keynes, "Æthelbald," 13–14.

apparent that Ælfwald's active interest in Guthlac stemmed from a common understanding of holiness amongst the Byzantine, Continental, and Insular Christians of the first millennium.

St. Guthlac of Crowland was an inspirational penitent, a famed counsellor to both royalty and commoners, and—like Cuthbert the Wonderworker—a beloved patron of animals.[47] The young Guthlac, of royal descent, won fame at the head of a Mercian war band whilst fighting the British on the borders of Wales, having been inspired by his pagan ancestors.[48] At the age of twenty-four, however, after reflecting on the common fate of worldly heroes, that is, corruption and death, he was moved in his spirit to turn to Christ—the Way, the Truth, and the Life (John 14:6). On entering the double-monastery at Repton, where he was trained by its holy abbess, Ælfthryth, he immediately became distinguished for his piety and asceticism, his incomparable gentleness eventually earning the affection of his jealous brethren.[49] In c. 700, Guthlac was stirred by the stories and sayings of the desert fathers to retreat to the wilderness to foster a more intimate relationship with our Lord through practical asceticism and contemplation.[50] He made his way to the marshland in the Eastern region of England known as the Fens, which constituted the border between the rival kingdoms of Mercia and East Anglia. Much like the deserts of Egypt, Asia Minor, and Mesopotamia, the Fens were a notorious breeding ground for demonic activity. The brave Guthlac set out to exorcise this ghostly wasteland in imitation of his saintly predecessors, building a shelter by cutting into the side of a Roman or British burial-mound where he lived austerely for the remainder of his life.[51]

With the assistance of the angels and his beloved patron, St. Bartholomew the Apostle, Guthlac overcame ghastly demons which took the shapes of disfigured men and wild animals, thus becoming the Mercian equivalent to Sts. Antony the Great and Cuthbert.[52] Guthlac soon became a healer and a prophet, his fame spreading throughout the different kingdoms of England only a generation later, thus contributing to their spiritual

47. For a summary of the holy ascetic's historical context, see Colgrave "Introduction" to *Felix's Life of St. Guthlac*, 1–7.

48. Felix, *Life of St. Guthlac* 16–18, 80–83.

49. Felix, *Life of St. Guthlac* 19–23, 82–87.

50. Felix, *Life of St. Guthlac* 24–26, 86–91.

51. Felix, *Life of St. Guthlac* 27–28, 90–95.

52. Felix, *Life of St. Guthlac* 29–34, 94–111.

unity. His transformation from chieftain to hermit is indeed quite striking. Rather than lead armies into battle to gain earthly treasures, Guthlac remained largely isolated from men in the company of angels and animals to arrive at union with God. He gave up the engraved armor and splendid garments to which he was entitled, preferring to wear simple tunics of hide. Instead of feasting at lavish banquets, he ate mere scraps of barley bread and drunk muddy water strictly after sundown.[53] He chose not to plunder his neighbors, but to trample on Satan and his servants through prayer and self-restraint. By the grace of God, even his temperament changed, his altruistic compassion substituting his ambitions and extending to the timidest creatures (typified by the little hirundines). The following story demonstrates how Guthlac arrived at the God-intended state of humanity before the ancestral fall, as a tender lord of creation:

> It is also pleasant to describe a spiritual miracle of Guthlac the most blessed servant of God. For it happened that on a certain day, while a venerable man named Wilfrid, who had long been bound by the bonds of spiritual friendship to Guthlac the man of God, was talking with him as was his custom, by chance two swallows suddenly entered his house: showing every sign of great joy, they opened their beaks and sang a song from their supple throats, as though they had arrived at their accustomed abode; without any hesitation they settled on the shoulders of the man of God Guthlac, and then chirping their little songs they settled on his arms, his knees, and his breast. Wilfrid was indeed amazed and, begging permission to speak, he began to ask how birds from the wild solitudes, unused to the approach of human beings, had the confidence to come near him. St. Guthlac answered him and said: "Have you not read how if a man is joined to God in purity of spirit, all things are united to him in God? and he who refuses to be acknowledged by men seeks the recognition of wild beasts and the visitations of angels; for he who is often visited by men cannot be often visited by angels." Then, taking a certain basket he placed one straw in it; and when the birds perceived this, as though they had been instructed by a familiar sign, they began to build a nest in it. And after about an hour had passed, when they had gathered together odds and ends and established a nest, St. Guthlac then placed the basket under the eaves of the dwelling in which he was sitting; and there the birds began to settle, having, as it were, acquired their own place of residence; but they did not

53. Felix, *Life of St. Guthlac* 28, 92–95.

> presume to choose a nesting-place without the permission of the
> man of God; and each year they came and sought from the man of
> God a sign to tell them where they were to dwell.[54]

In summary, there is much we can learn from the magnificent Celtic and Anglo-Saxon saints of our tradition. For instance, we can strive to imitate Cuthbert's steadfast patience and abounding compassion in times of personal illness and medical crises whilst imploring him to intercede for us, especially on his feast day, the 20th of March. Our father among the saints, Bede the Venerable, certainly expects us to do so given that Cuthbert was his beloved patron in this world, for whom he wrote no less than three biographies, including one in metrical verse.[55] Let us therefore remember to honor him too—particularly on the 27th of May—while following the example of his humility and spiritual discipline, as well as his full exploitation of his God-given charisms. Not all of us have been called to become staunch practical ascetics or highly eloquent contemplatives. Nonetheless, Bede, who is in the loving presence of God, will help us discover and use, for the benefit of the entire church, our spiritual gifts—whether these are of a practical or contemplative nature—through his intercessions. By asking Bede and his Insular forebears to pray for us, we will no doubt increase the likelihood of being taken up by our Lord and Savior, Jesus Christ, in a similar splendid manner at the respective ends of our lives. Moreover, we will appreciate the sheer blessing that it is to be children of God by adoption in a world called to be transfigured by his grace, as in the case of Guthlac. According to Felix, the eloquent East Anglian monk who composed Guthlac's *Vita*, the name of the Lord was always on the holy hermit's joyful lips, while his heart was filled with piety and his spirit was characterized by peace and mercy.[56] We should thus remember to commemorate our holy father, Guthlac, on the 11th of April, that we may receive but a fraction of his contentment, as well as his affection for animals and the environment. On a final note, let us proudly celebrate all our Insular fathers and mothers and reclaim their wonderful contributions to Orthodoxy and wider humanity, including their literary, artistic, and administrative prowess, their apostolic fearlessness, their mystical insight, and, most importantly, their perfect love for God and neighbor.

---

54. Felix, *Life of St. Guthlac* 39, 120–23.

55. See *Bedas metrische Vita sankti Cuthberti* (complete details within the bibliography). For an analysis of Bede's original verse composition, see Lapidge, "Bede's Metrical *Vita S. Cuthberti*," 77–94.

56. Felix, *Life of St. Guthlac* 51, 162–63.

10

The Timeless Wisdom of the
Life of St. Mary of Egypt

MARY OF EGYPT (SIXTH century) is one of the most celebrated saints of the Orthodox tradition whose memory survives thanks to our holy father, Sophronius, Patriarch of Jerusalem (late sixth to early seventh centuries).[1] Despite being known from only one work, Mary is commemorated multiple times throughout the year, specifically, April 1 and the fifth Thursday and Sunday of Great Lent. The *Life of St. Mary* is in fact read during the Thursday's Matins service, with half of it being recited after the third ode of the *Great Canon of Repentance* composed by St. Andrew of Crete (mid-seventh to early eighth centuries).[2] To be sure, the enigmatic ascetic, Mary, features as a chief intercessor among the saints in this masterful liturgical work. What is more, she is the only other woman besides the Theotokos to be given special reverence on Mount Athos.[3] The reader may fairly ask why this should be the case given that there are many other saints who have contributed more directly to the church's practices and doctrines. To answer this question, we need to systematically explore the *Life of St. Mary*, whose popularity was

1. McLees, "Marvelous Life of Patriarch Sophronius I, His Company of Saints, and the Fall of Byzantine Jerusalem," 61.

2. Thekla and Katherine "Life of Saint Mary of Egypt," 100; Greek Orthodox Archdiocese of America, "Sunday of St. Mary of Egypt," lines 1–10.

3. I am indebted to the Melbourne-based Serbian Orthodox iconographer, Mr. Petar Stefanovic, for this insight.

such among our Christian forebears that it was translated into Latin and, in turn, numerous Romance, Germanic, Celtic, and Slavic languages.[4] But first, a brief assessment of the life's renowned author is required for us to make sense of its wider spiritual and literary contexts.

St. Sophronius of Jerusalem is one of the most important figures in the history of the church, having led the Orthodox resistance against the imperial imposition of the heretical doctrine known as "Monoenergism."[5] As concerns our interpretation of the *Life of St. Mary*, Sophronius' formation is of crucial importance. In short, the church father was born at Damascus in c. 550. He was formally trained as a rhetorician and became a pupil of St. John Moschus, a Palestinian monk and hagiographer. After witnessing the ascetical practices of the Orthodox Egyptians during his travels with John, Sophronius embraced the angelic life at the Holy Monastery of St. Theodosius in Palestine. He also spent ten years at Sinai with his mentor before returning to Palestine, specifically the New Lavra in Judea. He was then forced back to Egypt due to the infamous Persian invasions of the Byzantine Empire. From Egypt, the church father travelled to Rome, where he gained allies against Monoenergism. After the repose of John, whom he buried on Mount Sinai, Sophronius went to North Africa, where he spent some time with Greek monks, among them his spiritual son, St. Maximus the Confessor. Having beseeched the Patriarch of Constantinople, Sergius, to rebuke Cyrus of Alexandria—the major proponent of the aforementioned heresy—Sophronius at last made his way back to Jerusalem, where he was elevated to the status of patriarch and continued to fight for the Orthodox faith despite the eventual capture of his city by Arab Muslims.[6]

---

4. McLees, "Marvelous Life of Patriarch Sophronius I," 61.

5. In short, this teaching—aimed at union with the Monophysites—undermined the church's belief in the Lord's complete assumption of our nature (except for sin) whilst fully retaining his divinity. More precisely, proponents of Monoenergism asserted that the Lord had only one (loosely defined) "theandric" activity, rather than one fully human and another entirely divine. This was problematic insofar as the church fathers maintained on the basis of divine revelation that the Lord healed whatever he assumed in his humanity. The notion of one "activity" or "energy" in Christ had other negative implications and led to the disastrous notion that the Incarnate Lord had only one divine "will." "Monothelitism," as it came to be known, was eventually defeated in the Byzantine tradition through the efforts of Sophronius' disciple, St. Maximus the Confessor. Allen, *Sophronius of Jerusalem and Seventh-Century Heresy*, 23–34; Allen and Neil, "Introduction" to *Maximus the Confessor and His Companions*, 1–21.

6. Sophronius of Jerusalem, *Sophronius of Jerusalem and Seventh-Century Heresy*, 15–21.

Throughout his travels, Sophronius used his literary-rhetorical training to compose a variety of panegyrical, poetical, polemical, and hagiographical works. Regarding his composition of saints' lives, the church father was no doubt influenced by his mentor, John, who, just prior to his response, had finished compiling a number of sayings and stories regarding the wonder-working monks of Palestine.[7] Concerning the *Life of St. Mary* specifically, Sophronius was indebted to an anonymous source that received the story from the successors of her discoverer, St. Zosimas of Palestine.[8] Our tradition has never denied the historicity of the life; however, it is evident that Sophronius has framed the narrative in a manner reminiscent of the spiritual classics of his time. He was no doubt exposed to the latter as a learned monk travelling around the major centers of the Roman Empire. We thus find echoes of the *Sayings of the Desert Fathers*, John's *Spiritual Meadow*, Jerome's *Life of St. Paul the Hermit*, and Cyril of Scythopolis' *Life of St. Kyriakos* in the *Life of St. Mary*.[9] Sophronius' purpose in alluding to these works was to place Mary and her interlocutor, Zosimas, in a tradition of holy elders that stemmed as far back as the second century. Moreover, we can assume that—as a saint with the charism of discernment—he chose to emphasize whatever aspects of the story he felt most benefited the faithful.

Moving on to his wonderful text, Sophronius begins the prelude by reflecting on his responsibility to "reveal gloriously the works of God" (Tob 12:7 LXX), admitting his fear to hide the story which he is about relate, represented as a "talent" bestowed by the Lord (Matt 25:18–25).[10] The church father introduces the protagonist and ultimate source of the story, namely, Zosimas the hieromonk: "a man renowned for his way of life and gift of words; from the days of his infant swaddling clothes he was reared in monastic trials of asceticism and good works."[11] Sophronius notes that Zosimas excelled in the ascetical life in one of the monasteries of Palestine; a region renowned for its saints, as emphasized by John Moschus in his *Spiritual Meadow*. According to Sophronius, Zosimas is just as proficient in practical asceticism as he is in contemplation, so that many come to him for spiritual counsel. He not only knows the Scriptures by heart but

---

7. Sophronius of Jerusalem, *Sophronius of Jerusalem and Seventh-Century Heresy*, 21–23; John Moschus, *Spiritual Meadow*.

8. Sophronius of Jerusalem, *Life of Saint Mary of Egypt*, 138.

9. Pepin and Feiss, *Saint Mary of Egypt*, 8–9.

10. Sophronius of Jerusalem, *Life of Saint Mary of Egypt*, 106.

11. Sophronius of Jerusalem, *Life of Saint Mary of Egypt*, 108.

embodies their teachings. Through naivety, or perhaps on account of pride, he begins to wonder if there is any monk on earth who remains to teach him something about the spiritual life. The thought serves as the catalyst for Zosimas's adventure; an angel appears and bids him to go to a secluded monastery beyond the Jordan River, that he may recognize other, more striking, ways that lead to salvation.[12]

Zosimas immediately displays courage and the virtue of obedience, leaving the only home that he has ever known. He reaches the said monastery and is welcomed by the abbot (later identified as "John"—not to be confused with Sophronius's mentor). He relates that he has come seeking spiritual profit, having heard of the abbot's skill in drawing souls to God. The abbot humbly admits him to the monastery, praying that Christ and the Holy Spirit will guide them both accordingly. The monastery consists of elders who are in fact more advanced in the spiritual life than Zosimas by all accounts. They keep constant vigil whilst standing, even throughout the night; they never speak an idle word; they have no worldly possessions or cares; they feed on bread and water and are for the most part sustained by the Word of God. Zosimas is edified in their presence, displaying the humility and courtesy characteristic of genuine monks. He dwells for some time in the monastery, which is generally locked; it is "a desert and not only out of reach for most of the neighboring monks but even unknown."[13]

Great Lent arrives and God's purpose in sending Zosimas out on his quest is made manifest. Following Holy Communion and a modest meal consisting of Lenten food, the brothers gather in the church, pray with prostrations, and then kiss and ask one another for forgiveness. Having received the blessing of the abbot, all but two monks venture out into the wilderness, chanting Ps 26. The two who remain are not meant to guard any property—since there is not much to speak of—but to ensure that the Divine Liturgy will continue to take place in the *katholikon* of the monastery. Most take with them the basic portions of food that their bodies require: bread, figs, dates, and wheat soaked in water. A few skilled in foraging, or perhaps more spiritually advanced, take nothing, choosing instead to rely on the plants of the desert. The brothers scatter and follow their standard rule in the wilds throughout Great Lent until Holy Week. More precisely, they do not talk to each other, neither do they enquire into how they are going to fast or survive. If the brothers happen to see each other during this

---

12. Sophronius of Jerusalem, *Life of Saint Mary of Egypt*, 109.

13. Sophronius of Jerusalem, *Life of Saint Mary of Egypt*, 109–11, esp. 111.

time, they run in opposite directions, choosing instead to live alone with God. This rule is comparable to Byzantine *xeniteia* and Irish *peregrinatio*. Zosimas imitates the example of his new brothers, secretly hoping to find a desert father who may enlighten him further.[14]

Zosimas travels and prays for twenty days, racing on as if he is going to a specific place. He takes small breaks from his journey by praying on his knees whilst facing the east at set times of the day. As he is praying at the sixth hour, he suddenly sees a figure to the right of the hillock that he is standing on. The figure is naked with short white hair and skin darkened by the sun. Zosimas crosses himself and sets out in pursuit of the stranger, believing that he has found a holy elder in the tradition of St. Macarius of Egypt. As he is gaining on the stranger, he asks why they are running from him, "an old man, a sinner."[15] He implores the stranger for the sake of the love of God to explain what they are doing in the desert. The stranger reveals that she is a woman and cannot turn to face Zosimas for the sake of pious modesty. She thus asks for his cloak, calling him by name.[16]

Zosimas is overcome with fear, realizing that the person whom he is speaking to has the gift of foresight. Having covered herself, the female hermit asks Zosimas what he should want to see, hear, or learn from her, particularly given his own progress in the ascetical life. This second indication of the hermit's spiritual insight prompts Zosimas to offer a prostration and ask for her blessing. The woman likewise bows low, so that they both lie

---

14. Sophronius of Jerusalem, *Life of Saint Mary of Egypt*, 111–13. In short, *peregrinatio* was largely a Western monastic phenomenon that consisted in perpetual exile from the comforts of this world, all of which were believed to pose a distraction to the spiritual life. It was therefore considered a type of martyrdom in which the faithful died to the world that they might live in and for Christ. It was particularly austere in the Irish context given the high value which the general society placed on familial ties, as well as its powerful sense of patriotism, predominately landed wealth, and various legal restrictions regarding travel. See Cutrer, "Early Irish *Peregrinatio* as Salvation History," 76–90. The Byzantines developed a similar notion of "wandering for the sake of God (ξενιτεία διὰ Θεόν)." However, both they and their Continental counterparts came to discourage this form of asceticism, likely owing to the increased use of the Rules of Basil and Benedict, which emphasised the importance of remaining within the context of a community for spiritual growth and stability. The Byzantine critics of such ascetical wandering termed its adherents "gyrovagues (κυκλεταί/*gyrovagi*)." See: McGuckin, "Aliens and Citizens of Elsewhere," 23–38, esp. 29; Ivanov, *Holy Fools in Byzantium and Beyond*, 64. Mary of Egypt, who roamed the desert and shunned all human contact until otherwise compelled by Divine Providence, is the most notable exception in this regard.

15. Sophronius of Jerusalem, *Life of Saint Mary of Egypt*, 113–16, esp. 116.

16. Sophronius of Jerusalem, *Life of Saint Mary of Egypt*, 116.

prostrate asking each other for a benediction. The hermit reminds Zosimas that it is his responsibility to offer the blessing and pray since he has been dignified by the order of the priesthood and preparing and distributing the body and blood of Christ for many years. She eventually consents to Zosimas' wish out of obedience and humility. Nevertheless, the hermit considers herself subject to his authority.[17] In highlighting this aspect of the ascetics' encounter, Sophronius is reminding us that the saints are always part of the hierarchical framework of the church, and never seek to assert their authority above it. At the same time, the wider church acknowledges the fact that Christ works directly through his saints, and they are subsequently able to console, correct, and intercede for the faithful. In other words, the hierarchical and the charismatic/prophetical traditions ultimately work in perfect harmony for the salvation of the world.

Mary's knowledge of Zosimas's name, vocation, and spiritual progress compels tears of compunction from him. Tears of compunction are indeed a sign of holiness according to the tradition of the desert fathers. We thus have here two saints in conversation. After both figures rise to their feet, the hermit again asks why Zosimas should wish to see someone not just sinful but "stripped of every virtue."[18] She nonetheless suggests that he has been sent to her through the grace of the Holy Spirit, to perform a special service for her in due course. Interestingly, the holy hermit enquires into how the kings are faring, and how the church is being guided. Zosimas responds that there has been lasting peace for both the church and the empire thanks to her prayers of intercession.[19] By emphasizing this aspect of the encounter, Zosimas is reiterating the church's conviction that the inhabited world, commonly termed *oikoumene* in Greek, is preserved through the prayers of the saints and the monks more generally. The monastic tradition is never isolated from the church or wider society.[20]

Zosimas asks the hermit to pray for him, prompting her to kindly protest once again that it is his responsibility as a presbyter. She nonetheless consents once more in obedience to his priestly authority. The hermit's prayers are inaudible and take quite long. Zosimas is thus compelled to lift his eyes from the ground. He sees the holy ascetic levitating from

---

17. Sophronius of Jerusalem, *Life of Saint Mary of Egypt*, 117–18.

18. Sophronius of Jerusalem, *Life of Saint Mary of Egypt*, 119.

19. Sophronius of Jerusalem, *Life of Saint Mary of Egypt*, 118–19.

20. See, for example: Serapion of Thmuis, *Letter to the Monks*, 70–71; Barsanuphius of Gaza and John the Prophet, *Letter 569*, 146–47.

the ground and, consumed by terror, is tempted to think that she is an evil spirit. The hermit, however, has the gift to read people's hearts. She turns and raises Zosimas, reassuring him that she is a human being, albeit a sinful one, by crossing her forehead, eyes, mouth, and heart. According to ascetical and hagiographical literature, the sign of the cross is a sure means of combatting demonic forces, hence our frequent use of it in our daily lives.[21] Moreover, the saint's proximity to the Lord during prayer accounted for her being elevated from the ground, thereby defying the natural laws of the fallen world.

The hermit implores God to defend humanity from the intense hatred of the ancestral enemy. Zosimas then beseeches her to reveal her story, stressing that God has sent him into the desert to find her and that she is obliged to reveal her story according to his will—otherwise she would have remained anonymous. She is persuaded to reveal her story yet first emphasizes the shameful nature of her past life, asserting that she was the "vessel of the devil."[22] She also asks Zosimas to pray for her. He weeps as she begins to narrate the course of her life.

The hermit reveals that she is a native of Egypt who renounced her loving parents at the tender age of twelve and went to Alexandria. We have here a trajectory all too familiar: a simple (likely village) life rejected for the so-called splendor and the temptations of the city. With shame, the ascetic recalls how she was immediately corrupted by the demon of lust. She engaged in fornication with many men unreservedly for seventeen years, considering this sad mode of being—whose ultimate outcome is death— "life . . ."[23] Despite her extreme poverty, she offered her body freely. We need to bear in mind that sexual promiscuity was not merely taboo but widely condemned during the Middle Ages. The maiden's passion therefore compelled her to become a social outcast. Certainly, it is a tremendous crime that lustful conduct is not merely tolerated in our day and age but widely celebrated. Lust serves as a means of social inclusion, while chastity is largely mocked. In fact, the only legitimate context for physical relations—that is, marriage between a man and a woman—is rapidly being dispensed with by non-Orthodox. This situation makes Mary's story all more the relevant to us, especially our youth, which is exposed to lustful imagery in an unprecedented manner by the entertainment and fashion industries.

21. Athanasius of Alexandria, *Greek Life of Antony*, 89, 91.
22. Sophronius of Jerusalem, *Life of Saint Mary of Egypt*, 119–21, esp. 121.
23. Sophronius of Jerusalem, *Life of Saint Mary of Egypt*, 121.

Returning to the story, the hermit goes on to relate how, during a certain summer, this catastrophic mode of existence was radically disrupted. In short, she saw a large throng of Libyans and Egyptians running towards the sea, venturing to Jerusalem for the feast of the Exaltation of the Precious and Lifegiving Cross. Tragically, she took the sacred celebration as an occasion to satisfy her sinful desire by corrupting young sailors. With much heartache, the hermit relates that she forcefully corrupted many men on the voyage, using her body to pay for it. The holy ascetic expresses her amazement that God allowed the boat to survive the journey yet at the same time speculates that the Lord mercifully permitted it with a view to her salvation. She underscores that the Lord "does not want the death of a sinner, but generously waits for [their] conversion."[24] Having arrived in Jerusalem, the young maiden continued to ensnare young men in the days leading up to the feast, both locals and foreigners.

Finally, the feast of the Exaltation arrived. The young maiden followed the crowd to the Church of the Holy Sepulcher. She struggled to make her way through the crowd until she reached the entrance. Strikingly, although everyone around her entered the church freely, the maiden was stopped in her tracks. An invisible force prevented her from moving beyond the doors. She tried to enter again three or four times after being brushed aside by the crowds, to no avail. She ultimately gave up on the porch.[25]

We can take it for granted that our Lord himself was directly behind the aforementioned "force," bearing in mind that it was his church, and it was he who sanctified the object of veneration to which the crowds were flocking. Truly, he used this object for our salvation. And yet the Lord was displaying great mercy in barring the entrance. His intention appears to have been to compel her to seek out his Mother, that she might pray to him for her sake. Sure enough, the young maiden realized this, having been moved in the heart by the Logos of salvation to weep, lament, and beat her breast whilst sighing from the depths of her heart before the icon of the Mother of God.[26]

The young maiden humbly entreated the Theotokos—her opposite in every way—for assistance, acknowledging her own unworthiness before the great Virgin. Interestingly, in her prayer to Panagia, the maiden demonstrates her knowledge of Christ's sacrifice and his purpose in suffering for our sake.

24. Sophronius of Jerusalem, *Life of Saint Mary of Egypt*, 121–23.

25. Sophronius of Jerusalem, *Life of Saint Mary of Egypt*, 123–25.

26. Sophronius of Jerusalem, *Life of Saint Mary of Egypt*, 125.

Later, the hermit implies that she had never entered a church before this time, so we can attribute such knowledge to word of mouth. At any rate, she vows to the Virgin that she will give up fornication entirely as soon as she may be permitted to venerate the holy cross, and that she will renounce the world and go wherever the holy mother should lead her.[27]

Surely, this came to pass, and the maiden returned to the icon to thank the Theotokos and fulfil her vow. She heard a voice from heaven saying, "If you cross the Jordan, you will find glorious peace."[28] Trusting wholly in the Theotokos, she set off on her journey. As she was leaving the city, a pious and mysterious stranger gave her three coins, which she then used to purchase three loaves of bread for her flight. In short, she received some directions from the baker to get her started and ran towards the Jordan with tears, eventually finding the way from passers-by. She visited the Church of St. John the Baptist on the banks of the Jordan—where she partook of the Holy Eucharist—before entering the wilderness. Having spent the night on the bank, and consumed half of one of her loaves, she found a small boat and crossed the river. All the while, she continued to pray to the Theotokos, her glorious patron. The hermit points out that she has remained in the wilderness alone since then, clinging to God.[29]

Zosimas is amazed to discover that the hermit has been living in the wilderness for forty-seven years, surviving initially on the limited loaves then whatever herbs she managed to find and, most importantly, contemplation. She also bravely endured the elements after her clothes completely wore out. Moreover, the hermit reveals all the temptations that she has experienced in the desert, including a longing for food, water, wine, and secular songs, as well her former lustful conduct. More importantly, the holy ascetic reveals how she was able to overcome such temptations, that is, through tears of compunction, prostrations, and prayers. In fact, she would lie prostrated for the duration of a whole night when needed. In such instances, she always threw herself before the Theotokos and—owing to the latter's intercessions—was consoled and encouraged by God's uncreated energies in the form of divine light.[30] She explicitly identifies her mystical sustenance: "I feed on and cover myself with the [W]ord of God, Lord of all. For not by bread alone will man live and all those having

<hr>

27. Sophronius of Jerusalem, *Life of Saint Mary of Egypt*, 125, 130.

28. Sophronius of Jerusalem, *Life of Saint Mary of Egypt*, 126.

29. Sophronius of Jerusalem, *Life of Saint Mary of Egypt*, 126–27.

30. Ware, *Orthodox Way*, 169–77.

no clothes will be clothed in stone, having discarded the outer covering of sin (Job 24; Heb 11:38)."[31]

Noting how the hermit has reiterated the Scriptures, Zosimas asks whether she has read the Psalms and related books. The hermit replies that she has never learned from books, nor heard from anyone for several decades. Rather, the Word of God—Christ himself—has directly instructed her.[32] We have an example of what scholars have termed "experiential epistemology" based on St. Maximus the Confessor's teachings and those of the enigmatic homilist of the fifth century known to posterity as "Macarius." In short, the monastic tradition has long maintained that genuine knowledge of God and his ways can be arrived at not only through discursive reasoning but through practical asceticism—consisting of fasting, prostrations, and acts of charity—and contemplation—including vigils and constant repetition of the Jesus Prayer.[33]

Zosimas is moved to bow down before the ascetic upon the conclusion of her story. Ever mindful of his sacred office, and her own need to cultivate humility, the hermit raises him once more, and begs him not to relate their encounter. Instead, she asks that the hieromonk not return to same spot the following year during Lent, nor sojourn in accordance with the custom of the monastery. In fact, she affirms that he will not be able to, again displaying her gift of foresight. Instead, she asks him to come to the banks of the Jordan the next year at sunset during Holy and Great Thursday and to bring the presanctified body and blood of the Lord (which she has not received since that lifesaving moment when she entered the wilderness). She also instructs him to inform his abbot, John, to look to himself and the brothers after their next encounter, when God should inspire him. The hermit asks for Zosimas' prayers and departs. He then bows down upon the spot where she stood before returning to the monastery.[34] Zosimas' reverence for the holy ascetic should not surprise us; he recognizes Christ working through the saint, and the Holy Spirit dwelling in her.

Zosimas keeps silent for the next year, longing to see the saint once more. When Great Lent comes, he is detained by an illness, thus fulfilling

---

31. Sophronius of Jerusalem, *Life of Saint Mary of Egypt*, 127–29, esp. 129.

32. Sophronius of Jerusalem, *Life of Saint Mary of Egypt*, 130.

33. See, for example, Tatakis, *Christian Philosophy in the Patristic and Byzantine Tradition*, 118–20; Aquino, *"Philokalia* and Regulative Virtue Epistemology," 240–51; Plested, "Ascetic Tradition," 164–176, esp. 171–72.

34. Sophronius of Jerusalem, *Life of Saint Mary of Egypt*, 130–31.

the hermit's prophecy. He recovers by Holy Thursday and makes for the banks of the Jordan at sunset, as per instruction. The hieromonk takes with him the presanctified gifts, together with a few figs and soaked lentils. When he reaches the banks of the river, he sits down and waits for the hermit. When she is late in coming, he begins to pray. Zosimas starts to doubt and is disturbed to realize that there is no boat with which the hermit may cross the river. As soon as these thoughts begin to fester, he sees the holy ascetic on the other side of the water.[35]

The hermit makes the sign of the cross over the Jordan, which is well lit by the moon. She begins walking across the surface of the river towards him.[36] The reference to the sign of the cross indicates that the hermit's power stems from Christ. The saints accomplish nothing by themselves. Their virtue stems from their utter surrender to Christ and their fulfilment of his will.

Zosimas' resulting attempt to prostrate himself, however, is rebuked by the hermit, who reminds him that he is carrying the body and blood of Christ. We have the church mother constantly prioritizing the sacraments and the priestly office above her own prophetical and wonderworking talents. She asks a trembling Zosimas to bless her. The church father marvels at the fact that purification coupled with God's grace has the power to transform the believer into a 'little Christ'. He at last realizes how far he is from perfection.[37]

The ascetics recite the Symbol of Faith and Lord's Prayer together and perform the customary kiss of peace. The hermit also recites St. Symeon's prayer—"Lord, now let your servant depart in peace . . ."—before asking Zosimas to return to his monastery.[38] She requests that he come to the place where they first met to see her again according to God's desire. The hieromonk expresses his pious affection for the saint, offering her some food. She takes merely three lentil pieces, affirming that the Holy Spirit nourishes and guards the substance of the soul. She asks Zosimas to pray for her. This repeated request on the part of the hermit shows that even the saints are dependent on the prayers of others. As is fitting, Zosimas asks her to pray for the church, the Roman Empire, and himself. The holy hermit leaves just

---

35. Sophronius of Jerusalem, *Life of Saint Mary of Egypt*, 131–33.
36. Sophronius of Jerusalem, *Life of Saint Mary of Egypt*, 133.
37. Sophronius of Jerusalem, *Life of Saint Mary of Egypt*, 133.
38. Sophronius of Jerusalem, *Life of Saint Mary of Egypt*, 133.

as she came. Zosimas returns to the monastery filled with joy yet regretting the fact that he has neglected to ask the saint her name.[39]

Another year passes and Zosimas ventures out into the desert once more. He reaches the spot where he first met the holy recluse but sees no sign of her. The hieromonk raises his eyes to heaven and prays for the Lord to reveal the saint. He then sees the body of the departed hermit on the opposite bank of the river, her face turned towards the rising sun. Her hands are crossed according to custom, and her face is turned to the east, the cardinal point associated with the resurrection. Zosimas runs up to her body and sheds tears over her feet. He also kisses them, not daring to touch any other part of the sacred vessel. The church father weeps for a long time before reciting the appointed psalms. Having read the relevant prayers for the departed, he asks himself whether he should bury the saint.[40] He then sees some words traced on the ground by her head:

> bury in this place the body of humble Mary, return dust to dust, having prayed to the Lord for me who died on the first day of the Egyptian month of Pharmuti, called April by the Romans, on the self-same night as the Lord's Passion, after making her communion of the Divine and Mysterious Supper.[41]

One may presume that the holy hermit was given the name "Mary" with the sacrament of baptism early in life, hence her capacity to partake of Holy Communion immediately following her conversion. Her name may also account for her special connection with Panagia. At any rate, Zosimas is happy to discover the name and moved to learn that the saint was mysteriously transported from the Jordan to the place of her repose—a spot twenty days away by his reckoning—as soon as she partook of the divine mysteries.[42]

Zosimas is faced with another challenge, that is, how to dig a grave in the dry and solid ground without an appropriate tool; all he has at his disposal is a small piece of wood left behind by some desert traveler. After a fair amount of toil, Divine Providence intervenes, and a lion comes to venerate Mary's body. This was by no means a new phenomenon. St. Antony the Great witnessed the same thing when attempting to bury his elder, St. Paul the Hermit. Zosimas is initially gripped by terror, recalling

39. Sophronius of Jerusalem, *Life of Saint Mary of Egypt*, 133–35.
40. Sophronius of Jerusalem, *Life of Saint Mary of Egypt*, 135–36.
41. Sophronius of Jerusalem, *Life of Saint Mary of Egypt*, 136.
42. Sophronius of Jerusalem, *Life of Saint Mary of Egypt*, 136.

that Mary had said that she had never encountered any animals in the wilderness. He nonetheless draws courage from her holy relics and commands the animal to assist him. In a manner reminiscent of Paul's burial, the lion digs a hole deep enough for the body.[43]

The miracle just described reflects the restoration of human nature on the part of both Mary and Zosimas in and through Christ. In short, St. Gregory of Nyssa, St. John Chrysostom, and other church fathers have outlined how the animals imitated the disobedience of Adam and Eve after the fall. Humans thus lost their privileged status as lords of creation when they introduced sin and death into the world. This was remedied by the Logos, who assumed and healed our humanity and placed it on the right hand of God the Father in fulfilment of his divine plan. The Lord then invited us to participate in his redemption of the cosmos more generally, and this has been reflected in the lives of many holy hermits from the Greek East and Latin West throughout the centuries, particularly their paradisal relations with animals and the elements. In drawing a lion to her departed body, Mary can be considered a "New Eve" like Panagia. In commanding a lion to bury the body, Zosimas may be considered a "New Adam" like Christ. Indeed, the lion expresses affection for both saints, revealing them to be true stewards of the created order.

Before laying Mary's body in the grave, Zosimas washes her feet with his tears. He then calls on her to pray for all. The lion goes off into the desert like a lamb whilst Zosimas returns to his monastery, glorifying our Savior. He then reveals his encounters with Mary to Abba John and the brethren, repeating her warning to the former. Sophronius relates that John went on to correct the brothers with God's help before disclosing how Zosimas departed this world near the age of one hundred. Sophronius affirms that the following generations of monks have preserved the story, which he is the first to transcribe. Before the text concludes with a

43. Sophronius of Jerusalem, *Life of Saint Mary of Egypt*, 136–37; Cf. Jerome of Stridon, *Vita beati Pauli monachi Thebaei* [i.e., *Life of St. Paul the Hermit*] 16, 176–80. In short, Jerome records in the *Life of St. Paul the Hermit* 16 that two male lions hurried to the subject's cell upon his death as Antony mourned that he did not have the necessary tools with which to bury him. The lions display great reverence for Paul's body and accomplish the task of digging his grave. Jerome describes how Antony was initially terrified at the sight of the animals but managed to perceive them as harmless as doves as soon as he focused his mind on God. The lions then seek Antony's blessing with prostrations, causing the Egyptian monk to praise Christ that even "mute animals (*muta animalia*)" acknowledge God's existence. Antony recites a brief prayer which emphasises Christ's compassionate care over trees and birds before blessing and dismissing the creatures.

doxology by a second, anonymous scribe, the righteous hierarch offers the following benediction: "And may God, who renders great things to those who seek Him, grant benefit to those who read this story as a reward for him whom He ordered to write it . . ."[44]

In recording the encounters between Zosimas and Mary, Sophronius has offered us two great intercessors before our Lord and Saviour, Jesus Christ. Mary in particular serves as the paradigm for penitents—*par excellence*. This applies to those who have been raised in the church and often fall despite their best attempts to remain faithful, and those who have converted to Orthodoxy at a mature change and continue to struggle against the bad habits cultivated in their past lives. Zosimas, too, can inspire us by his humility, best evidenced by his willingness to acknowledge how a former harlot surpassed him in virtue because of her ability—through God's merciful initiative and guidance—to renounce her sinful ways and depend entirely on the Lord and Panagia for her survival.

Furthermore, by framing the narrative in the manner described above, and by drawing on the wider hagiographical genre and his own insights as a holy hierarch, Sophronius reminds us that there are personal and corporate dimensions to our salvation. On the one hand, like Mary, we need to cultivate a living relationship with our saintly intercessors to overcome our wicked habits and temptations and arrive at union with God. On the other hand, we are obliged to honour and submit to the hierarchical framework of the church to retain our humility, acknowledging that it is inherently sacred since it has been established by Christ himself. Most importantly, we are utterly dependent on the sacrament of Holy Communion for our spiritual and physical sustenance, bearing in mind that the body and blood of the Lord will admit us into his eternal kingdom, as it did the holy hermit. If Mary was unwilling to depart this life without receiving the Eucharist despite her experience of the divine light, how much more should we desire it! On a final note, let us remember to imitate the zealous asceticism of Mary and Zosimas, that we may cultivate the same ardent affection for the Lord and his saints, especially our Panagia. May we have their loving prayers before the throne of Christ.

44. Sophronius of Jerusalem, *Life of Saint Mary of Egypt*, 137–38, esp. 138.

11

St. Maximus the Confessor on Love and Deification

For nothing is more truly Godlike than divine love, nothing more mysterious, nothing more apt to raise up human beings to deification. For it has gathered together in itself all good things that are recounted by the *logos* of truth in the form of virtue, and it has absolutely no relation to anything that has the form of wickedness, since it is the fulfilment of the law and the prophets.—St. Maximus the Confessor, *Letter 2: On Love.*[1]

OUR FATHER AMONG THE saints, Maximus, was born to a wealthy family in Constantinople in the late sixth century. After receiving an eminent education, he served as the private secretary of the emperor Heraclius and his grandson, Constans II. The Confessor abandoned his administrative career when he perceived that members of the Byzantine court were lapsing into heresies that denied our Lord's full humanity to contrive union with a large group of schismatics located on the Eastern fringe of the empire. In short, these false teachings culminated in what is known as Monothelitism, which contradicted our Lord's saving dispensation, i.e., his assumption and healing of the faculty of the will and, therefore, everything that pertains to human nature (while remaining free from sin). Maximus found refuge in the Holy Monastery of Chrysopolis (Skutari), where he became abbot and served the wider flock through his profound letters and

1. Maximus the Confessor, *Letter 2: On Love*, 85.

theological treaties. He was eventually forced to migrate to Africa owing to the infamous invasion of the Persians. Maximus ultimately succeeded St. Sophronius of Jerusalem in the Orthodox refutation of Monothelitism, obtaining assistance in Rome from Sts. Theodore and Martin (whom we likewise celebrate as confessors). The church father was eventually captured by the Monothelite authorities and condemned to death in exile in what is now Georgia (after his tongue and right hand were cruelly severed).[2] His position was formally vindicated by the church in Constantinople at the Sixth Ecumenical Council.[3] Having had a tremendous influence on the spiritual life and doctrinal understanding of every subsequent generation of the church, he remains the pride of the Byzantine tradition and a central figure in the history of Orthodoxy more generally.[4]

The striking passage cited above attests to the relationship between deification and altruistic conduct. It is deeply associated with Maximus' understanding of asceticism and the Lord's reiteration of the greatest commandments: "You shall love the Lord your God with all your heart, with all your soul, and with all your mind" and "You shall love your neighbor as yourself (Matt 22:37–40 NKJV)." Maximus addressed the letter to certain spiritual children of his in Constantinople.[5] He begins the epistle by commending his disciples for maintaining a loving disposition towards God and among themselves in his absence.[6] It is noteworthy that love—that is, *agape*—is the surest path to God according to Maximus. It is in no way a passive condition but a call to action.[7] This attitude is reflected elsewhere in the Confessor's writings, specifically in his *Four Hundred Texts on Love*, where he states that the compassionate disposition "may be recognized in the giving of money, and still more in the giving of spiritual counsel and in looking after people in their physical needs."[8] Maximus perceives love as the goal and content of preaching, the

2. Allen and Neil, *Life of Maximus the Confessor*, 38–185; Cf. Louth, "Introduction" to *Maximus the Confessor*, 3–18; Allen, "Life and Times of Maximus the Confessor," 3–18.

3. Allen and Neil, "Introduction" to *Maximus the Confessor and His Companions*, 29–30.

4. As attested to by the church father's prominent place in *Philokalia*, i.e., the collection of texts by Greek masters of the hesychastic tradition ranging from the fourth to fifteenth centuries. See: Maximum the Confessor, *Philokalia*, Vol. 2, 48–305.

5. Louth, "Introduction" to Maximus the Confessor, *Letter 2: On Love*, 84.

6. Maximus the Confessor, *Letter 2: On Love*, 85.

7. Tatakis, *Christian Philosophy in the Patristic and Byzantine Tradition*, 106.

8. Maximus the Confessor, *Four Hundred Texts on Love* 1.26, 55.

height of asceticism, and the perfection of the mind/soul.[9] Interestingly, Maximus also reveals in this letter the significance of kind-heartedness for those of us hoping to remedy the egocentrism, conflict, and loneliness characteristic of our secular society:

> Love alone, properly speaking, proves that the human person is in the image of the Creator, by making his self-determination submit to reason, not bending reason under it, and persuading the inclination to follow nature and not in any way to be at variance with the *logos* of nature. In this way we are all, as it were, one nature, so that we are able to have one inclination and one will with God and with one another, not having any discord with God or one another . . .[10]

One may ask at this point what Maximus meant by the expression "divine love" referred to above. In short, the Confessor has identified multiple gradations of love in his works, the most commendable (and, indeed, holy) being that which is entirely selfless and therefore directed towards everyone, including a person's enemies.[11] The importance that the Confessor places on loving all people equally is also reflected in his *Four Hundred Texts*. Having outlined how God, in his goodness and freedom from passion, loves all people to the same extent as his creatures—but glorifies the righteous—the church father asserts, "Similarly, a man of good and dispassionate judgement also loves all men equally [. . .]; and he loves the sinner, too, because of his nature and because in his compassion he pities him for foolishly stumbling in darkness."[12] The saint's general understanding of love appears to be based on the Lord's Sermon on the Mount:

> You have heard that it was said, "You shall love your neighbor and hate your enemy." But I say to you, love your enemies, bless those who curse you, do good to those who hate you, and pray for those who spitefully use you and persecute you, that you may be sons of your Father in heaven; for He makes His sun rise on the evil and on the good, and sends rain on the just and on the unjust [. . .]. Therefore, you shall be perfect, just as your Father in heaven is perfect (Matt 5:43–45, 48 NKJV).

9. Wessel, "Theology of *Agape* in Maximus the Confessor," 322.

10. Maximus the Confessor, *Letter 2: On Love*, 86–87.

11. Wessel, "Theology of *Agape* in Maximus the Confessor," 324–25.

12. Maximus the Confessor, *Four Hundred Texts on Love* 1.25, 55.

We may therefore conclude that Maximus believed that being godlike/deified consists in loving all people equally regardless of their righteous or sinful conduct. The Confessor maintained that all people deserve to be respected insofar as they have been created in God's image and likeness (Gen 1:26–27). More to the point, everyone has been called to participate in God's grace and the sinfulness that we may perceive in each other—whilst it is to be eschewed in every way—is not ours to condemn. Once again, this understanding can be related to our Savior's exhortations, chiefly: "be merciful, just as your Father also is merciful (Luke 6:36 NKJV)." Subsequently, the Confessor held that those who continue to distinguish their brothers and sisters in Christ based on their respective merits and flaws have not yet risen to the paradisal/perfect state and egalitarian outlook that this entails, especially as concerns the inherent existential value of every person owing to their common nature and origin.[13]

Yet love, according to Maximus, no longer comes naturally due to the ancestral fall (Gen 3). It is now the result of ascetical labor and prayerful contemplation, which help us rise above earthly distractions, and which the Confessor himself intensely experienced as a devoted monk. Monastic life no doubt informed Maximus' entire thought.[14] The link between the ascetical/virtuous life, love, and deification in the Confessor's writings may once again be verified by his *Four Hundred Texts*: "He who has genuinely renounced worldly things, and lovingly and sincerely serves his neighbour, is soon set free from every passion and made a partaker of God's love and knowledge."[15] In other words, the Confessor taught that we are called to transform our passions through practical asceticism—considered in terms of the rejection of base interests, on the one hand, and selfless conduct, on the other—that we may no longer harbor the feelings of resentment that prevent us from exercising mercy and compassion; that preclude us from imitating and coming to know our Lord Jesus Christ.

Subsequently, the Confessor teaches us that asceticism is not to be undertaken simply for the benefit of oneself. It is most certainly essential for our salvation; however, it is not a goal in itself. Neither does it imply a state of serenity for the human person in which they become aloof to the anxieties, needs, and spiritual struggles of others. Love for Christ and compassion

---

13. Wessel, "Theology of *Agape* in Maximus the Confessor," 326.

14. Meyendorff, *Byzantine Theology*, 72; Russell, *Doctrine of Deification in the Greek Patristic Tradition*, 262.

15. Maximus the Confessor, *Four Hundred Texts on Love* 1.27, 55.

for our fellow human beings manifested in prayer and action are the means by which we may redeemed in conjunction with God's grace.[16] We may thus appreciate why the Confessor insists in *Letter 2* that the human and the divine converge "through the unifying function of love [which is] the greatest of goods . . ."[17] Maximus certainly demonstrated this throughout the course of his life, even during the mock trial that he endured at the hands of the Monothelites. In fact, the *Record of the Trial (Relatio motionis)* defines Christian identity in terms of altruistic behavior and unerring loyalty to the Lord even amid persecution through its depiction of the Confessor and his disciple, St. Anastasius the Monk.

In brief, the anonymous author of the *Record* has related how Maximus prostrated himself and wept before his accusers throughout his ordeal without ever displaying signs of anger.[18] At one point the Confessor even stated that he would submit to punishment if the accusations of treason made against him could be proven.[19] This was in sharp contrast to his major accuser, the finance minister of the imperial capital, whose irascible behavior was reminiscent of the pagan authorities of Late Antiquity.[20] For the modern reader, the Confessor's weeping may seem confusing, particularly in light of the fact that the text highlights his innocence. Crying is not typically considered a heroic trait in our society, often reflecting a person's guilt or cowardice. However, this was not commonly the case for our Orthodox forebears. In the *Sayings of the Desert Fathers*, for instance, weeping is considered a sign of meekness, an indication that a person is holy and will thus "inherit the earth" (Matt 5:5 NKJV). This is demonstrated in the following story concerning two of the greatest ascetics from the mid-fourth to mid-fifth centuries, Sts. Arsenius and Poemen:

> It was said of him [i.e., Arsenius] that he had a hollow in his chest channelled out by the tears which fell from his eyes all his life while he sat at his manual work. When Abba Poemen learned that he was dead, he said weeping, "Truly you are blessed, Abba Arsenius, for you wept for yourself in this world! He who does not weep for himself here below will weep eternally hereafter; so

16. Meyendorff, *Byzantine Theology*, 71–72.

17. Russell, *Doctrine of Deification in the Greek Patristic Tradition*, 265.

18. *Relatio motionis* [i.e., *Record of the Trial*] 2, 4, and 7, 52–55, 64–65.

19. *Record of the Trial* 1, 50–51.

20. *Record of the Trial* 1, 2, and 4, 48–51; 58–59.

it is impossible not to weep, either voluntarily or when compelled through suffering."[21]

It is known that the tradition of the desert fathers was highly valued by Maximus.[22] It is possible that the enigmatic disciple who recorded the Confessor's hearing was aware of how it had influenced him. In any case, it is reasonable to assume that they intentionally portrayed the saint as a successor to the early martyrs and monks by drawing attention to his meekness and unshakable love for Christ; the latter best evidenced by his gracious yet resolute defiance of those who would dare to question the existence the Lord's human will. It is noteworthy that the Confessor was charged with hating the Monothelite authorities during his trial. Appealing to the Lord's instruction regarding the proper attitude that we should display towards our enemies, Maximus responded that he loved his heretical opponents on the basis of a shared language (and, by extension, culture), knowing full well that they would torment and exile him.[23] We see, then, how the great Byzantine theologian's teachings stemmed from authentic ascetical experience and *Christomimesis*. May we remember his discernment, courage, and perfect love for God and neighbor, both now and always.

21. *Sayings of the Desert Fathers*, 18.

22. Louth, "Recent Research on St Maximus the Confessor," 73.

23. *Record of the Trial* 11, 70–71.

12

St. Andrew of Crete's Adaptation
of the Scriptures

WITHOUT A DOUBT, OUR Byzantine forebears acknowledged the centrality of the Scriptures within tradition. Yet they also demonstrated flexibility in their interpretive approach, exploring various ways in which the Old and New Testaments may be reiterated for our salvation. Besides composing Biblical homilies in imitation of the early church fathers (such as St. John Chrysostom), Byzantine theologians developed short hymns known as *troparia* from the Scriptures and incorporated these within the liturgical framework, specifically in the hope of further enlightening the faithful. St. Andrew of Crete, a celebrated hymnographer, homilist, and hagiographer of the late-seventh to early-eighth centuries, is a notable example in this regard. The monastic bishop composed his *Great Canon of Repentance* as an invitation for us to consider numerous figures of salvation history as symbolizing many facets of our respective spiritual lives. It is reasonable to assume that the church father made the hymns succinct so that we may effectively memorize them, thus absorbing their salvific content.

When we perform Andrew's liturgical poetry in the first and last weeks of Great Lent, we repeatedly declare ourselves amongst the worst sinners that the world has ever known, confessing our sins to the Lord so that he may heal our spiritual infirmities. It ought to be emphasized that Andrew has ensured that his work is ultimately uplifting, comforting us as early as the twelfth *troparion* of the first ode. Here, the church father brilliantly associates the parable of the lost son with St. Paul's description of the Incarnate Lord as the epitome of God's mercy and affection: "Although I have sinned, O Saviour, yet I know that thou art lover of man: your chastisement is merciful, and fervent your compassion: you see the tears and hasten, as the Father, calling the prodigal" (Luke 15:11–32; Titus 3:4).[1]

Andrew encourages us to return to Christ in a spirit of meekness throughout the *Canon*. For example, he imitates the humility of the apostle Paul in the third *troparion* of the second ode, together with that of King David: "I have sinned above all men, alone I have sinned against you: but as you are God, O Saviour, have pity on your creation" (1 Tim 1:15; Ps 50:6 LXX; Matt 9:6).[2] The church father subsequently challenges us to seek redemption in the manner of the tax collector, at the same time warning us against the pride and hardheartedness of Pharisees such as Simon (Luke 7:36–50, 18:9–14).[3] The former aspect is illustrated in the twenty-fourth *troparion* of the second ode: "Be merciful, as the Publican, I cry unto you, O Saviour, be merciful to me: for there is none out of Adam, who has sinned, as I have, against you" (Luke 18:13).[4]

Penance for Andrew consists in humble introspection, his *Canon* constantly compelling us to identify our sinful habits and our postlapsarian tendency towards irascibility and concupiscence. The hymnographer assists us in this endeavor by offering other examples of reformed sinners and saints featured within the Holy Writ, ranging from the Patriarch Abraham (a symbol of resolution) to the penitent thief on the cross (an image of ardent faith).[5] Exemplars like the latter especially console us by reminding us that our fallen condition is not unique; that we are all subject to the same temptations, yet capable of overcoming these by the grace of the Godman. As a matter of fact, Andrew explicitly identifies his pastoral aim within the twelfth *troparion* of the eighth ode, and in the fourth hymn of the ninth. The saint affirms that our church is defined by moral standards, forever promoting "the pious deeds of the righteous," which obviously involve a certain degree of diligence.[6] According to Andrew, it is not a matter of cultivating *accidie* (i.e., listlessness that leads to despair) when we fall (as it may be today

---

1. Andrew of Crete, *Great Canon*, 48.

2. Andrew of Crete, *Great Canon*, 52.

3. Andrew of Crete, *Great Canon*, 95.

4. Andrew of Crete, *Great Canon*, 54.

5. Andrew of Crete, *Great Canon*, 61, 96.

6. Andrew of Crete, *Great Canon*, 88.

for other denominations), but of regaining "the mercy of Christ, through prayer and fasting, purity and soberness" (Matt 9:15; 1 Pet 4:7).[7]

The didactic function of the *Great Canon* is demonstrated in the seventh *troparion* of the first ode, where the saint equates our misuse of the gift of freewill with self-destruction. In this verse, in which Andrew has appealed to the language of St. Peter, we are exhorted to ponder discernment as the ultimate victim of irrational impulses inevitably expressed in action: "I have walked in the footsteps of blood-thirsty Cain, by deliberate choice, giving life to the flesh, becoming the murderer of the conscience of my soul and warring upon it by my evil deeds" (Gen 4:8; 1 Pet 2:11).[8] The hymnographer intimates that unbridled anger and desire (typified by Cain) hinder genuine examination of the soul called to be innocent (tacitly represented by Abel), thus separating us from Christ, our prototype.

The church father identifies the Lord as our existential model in the fifth hymn of the ninth ode whilst citing the self-emptying and self-sacrifice love that he illustrated through his birth and ministry: "Christ became a child, associated to me in the flesh, and he fulfilled by will, all that pertains to nature, save sin alone: a pattern for you, O soul, and image presenting his condescension" (Matt 1:25; Luke 2:7; Heb 2:17, 4:15).[9] "Condescension" is the literal English rendering of the Greek noun *synkatabasis*, expounded upon by Chrysostom in relation to our Savior. It is not at all patronizing, instead denoting God's gracious acceptance of our limitations, i.e., our mortality through the incarnation, and our limited capacity to describe him as the eternal Word (together with the Father and the Holy Spirit) following revelation, as with the Scriptures.[10] We are therefore called to be patient with ourselves, always remembering Christ's longsuffering towards humanity.

It significant that the holy hierarch ultimately disapproves the state of guilt, presenting it as something unwelcome and unpleasant, a direct result of unnatural behavior. More precisely, in the twentieth hymn of the ninth ode, he warns the soul not to show itself "worse through despair" but to have "the faith of the Canaanite woman, through which her daughter was healed" and cry to the Lord "save me also, Son of David" (Matt

---

7. Andrew of Crete, *Great Canon*, 92–93.

8. Andrew of Crete, *Great Canon*, 47.

9. Andrew of Crete, *Great Canon*, 93; Andrew of Crete, *Magnus Canon* (PG 97, 1381A).

10. Hill, "Introduction" to John Chrysostom, *Homilies on Genesis 1–17*, 17–18.

15:21–28).[11] Andrew undoubtedly maintained that excessive remorse can result in *accidie* for those who do not recognize God's benevolence, having been influenced by his ascetical forebears during his formation at the monastery of St. Sava in Jerusalem.

Throughout the *Canon*—which offers public confession to the entire congregation—the church father juxtaposes regret with hope, as in the verse: "Have mercy, O Lord, have mercy upon me, I cry to you, when you will come with your Angels, to render to all in the measure of their deeds" (Matt 16:27).[12] It is important to bear in mind that the courageous cry of such a humbling petition on the part of the blind beggar, Bartimaeus, caught the attention of the Lord amongst the crowds on the road to Jericho, and led to the restoration of his sight (Mark 10:46–52; Luke 18:35–43). Hence, in the sixteenth *troparion* of the ninth ode, Andrew credits the salvation of the publican and the purification of the harlot with the alabaster jar of myrrh to its heartfelt recitation (Luke 7:47–50, 18:10–14).[13] His approach towards grief is entirely consistent with that of the desert fathers of Late Antiquity, especially Abba Hyperechius, who affirmed that the devoted Christian (represented by the figure of the monk) "transforms the night into day by keeping watch and assiduously persisting in prayers. Goading his heart, he pours forth tears and calls forth mercy from on high."[14]

God-inspired compunction is but one aspect of the *Great Canon*. There are also moral exhortations drawn from the stories of the Old and New Testaments urging the reader to flee from sin. Take, for example, the fifteenth *troparion* after the second *Irmos* (i.e., thematical and metrical link) of the third ode, which pertains to bodily desires: "As Lot did the fire, so you my soul flee from sin: flee Sodom, and Gomorrah, flee the flame of every inordinate lust" (Gen 19:15–22).[15] Another call to action is featured within the fifth ode, where Andrew instructs us to approach Christ despite our uncleanness just like the bleeding woman who had likely been ostracized from her community owing to the ceremonial defilement presented by her affliction (Lev 15:25–30).[16] More precisely, the church father adjures: "Follow, O wretched soul, the woman with an issue

---

11. Andrew of Crete, *Great Canon*, 95.

12. Andrew of Crete, *Great Canon*, 62.

13. Andrew of Crete, *Great Canon*, 95.

14. *Book of the Elders*, 32.

15. Andrew of Crete, *Great Canon*, 62.

16. *Orthodox Study Bible*, 1284.

of blood: run quickly, grasp the hem of Christ, that scourging the stream [of sin] you may hear from him: your faith has saved you" (Matt 9:20–22; Mark 5:25–34; Luke 8:43–48).[17]

Andrew formed his *Great Canon* from the Scriptures because they present existential paradigms essential for our journey to the kingdom, their historicity notwithstanding. I have barely scratched the surface of this work, which is amongst the longest of our liturgical services. Much can be said concerning its significance for Great Lent, and of its theological and exegetical import more generally.[18] My intention has been to demonstrate that our Byzantine forebears successfully interiorized the Word of God, using both the Old and New Testaments to enrich other forms of artistic expression, thereby imbuing the minds of the faithful with their unique imagery and phraseology. It must be noted that such appropriation has not been limited to liturgical poetry throughout the ages, having extended to biography, history, and the visual arts.

Due to the ascetical and literary efforts of paragons like Andrew, the Word of God continues to rehabilitate and reassure us in ways that are both practical and aesthetically engaging. Those who have not earnestly participated in our liturgical services cannot understand the significance of this development in the history of worship. Overemphasizing the historical dimension of the Scriptures—and having no grasp of the spiritual due to a severe lack of *askesis* and contemplation—many other traditions sadly do not appreciate our use of them as a language of devotion. We are in fact very blessed to comprise the Orthodox Church, which affords us not only the proper context in which to repent our sins and celebrate our intercessors before Christ but also the correct manner. This largely consists in the appropriation of the Scriptures in moving melodies, as promoted by Andrew. Let us therefore remember to attend the Divine Liturgy on our beloved father's feast day (the 4th of July) so that we may joyfully liken him to the psalmist for having composed "a new song in the assembly of the righteous" and "thundered forth [. . .] hymns of grace and the Word of righteousness for our salvation . . ."[19]

17. Andrew of Crete, *Great Canon*, 73.

18. See, for example, Harkianakis, "Ποίηση καὶ Δόγμα εἰς τὸ ἔργο τοῦ ἁγίου Ἀνδρέου Κρήτης," 316–27.

19. Irvin, *Hours*.

13

Life in the Spirit: Insights from
St. Symeon the New Theologian

BORN TO A PRIVILEGED family in the late tenth century, the boy destined to earn the unique and distinguished title of "New Theologian" was baptized "George" and sent to study in Constantinople. Despite familial ties with the ruling elite, and the talent to pursue a more rigorous education, George sought out a more spiritual life in his early teens, disillusioned as he was with the immoral behavior that characterized such persons as the reigning emperor, Romanos II. To this end, the young man entrusted himself to an unordained monk of the Studion monastery named "Symeon"—later known to tradition as "the Pious." Although he had been afforded a vision of the elder surrounded by divine light in response to his prayer to discover a saintly mentor, George briefly returned to his worldly career. Through the elder's intercessions, however, he ultimately entered the Studion monastery as a postulant. Regrettably, George and his spiritual father had their share of critics which attempted to disrupt their bond in the Lord; the latter possibly having been a "fool for Christ," hence his being treated with suspicion. George was thus admitted with the help of Symeon to the Holy Monastery of St. Mamas located nearby, at which he was rapidly tonsured, ordained, and appointed abbot. It is here that he took on the name of his spiritual father—who continued to serve as his guide—seeking to inspire the same contemplation in his monks which had facilitated his own mystical experiences, and which had already resulted in a dynamic, living relationship with the Risen Lord.[1]

As is always the case with God's elect, the younger Symeon was obliged to contend against the ancestral enemy, who inspired envy in his fellow monastics and clergymen. Sadly, many within the ecclesiastical framework had become hardhearted and Pharisaic by this time, so that they resented the church father's reputation for holiness and many charisms. The latter consisted in his homiletics, hymnody, and capacity to perceive the saintliness of others, most especially his mentor. Although the patriarch of Constantinople had hitherto supported the younger Symeon whenever such matters came to a head, the hierarch's *synkellos* (secretary), Stephen—who had previously been Metropolitan of Nicomedia—managed to convene a Synod that condemned the New Theologian to exile. Symeon's major "crimes" according to the assembly were that he had been annually celebrating the memory of his eponymous elder in the Divine Liturgy and commissioning and venerating icons of the latter. By God's grace, the church father found refuge in an oratory dedicated to St. Marina on land belonging to one of his spiritual children. Symeon had acquired the respect of many nobles by this time who eventually convinced the patriarch to rescind the decision of the mock synod, so that the New Theologian was permitted to openly honor his spiritual father once more. He returned to the oratory of Marina with his closest disciples, where he lived until his departure from this world, completing his celebrated hymns in peace.[2]

Symeon's most profound work consists in his *Discourses*, recited and recorded during his tenure as abbot of the Monastery of St. Mamas. In short, these were originally delivered to his monks during their Matins services. Hortatory and highly personal in nature, the *Discourses'* content varies depending on the liturgical period or specific feast which occasioned them, but we may discern two major themes throughout the collection. The first is the need for practical asceticism and contemplation to arrive at a genuine understanding of, and communion with, God, as articulated by great saints like Maximus the Confessor. The second consists in an emphasis on the activity of the Holy Spirit, who effects the ascetical

---

1. Niketas Stethatos, *Life of Saint Symeon the New Theologian* 1–30, 1–67; Hunt, *Guide to St. Symeon the New Theologian*, 1–7; Turner, "Introduction" to Symeon the New Theologian, *Epistles of St. Symeon the New Theologian*, 1–4.

2. Niketas Stethatos, *Life of Saint Symeon the New Theologian* 74–108,167–251; Hunt, *Guide to St. Symeon the New Theologian*, 7–16; Turner, "Introduction" to *Epistles of St. Symeon the New Theologian*, 4–6.

life in the first instance, and who serves as the remedy to all religious formalism that might stifle the dynamism of the gospel. Subthemes include penitence, dispassion, and charity.[3]

Discourse 15 is particularly interesting given the antithesis which the church father presents herein between the true experience of holiness and the skepticism that this is often met with, as in the case of his spiritual father and the Stoudion monks. Symeon begins by comparing the carnal mindedness of the opponents of the Christian faith throughout the ages with that of Adam, who had "fallen from the knowledge and contemplation of God" after having "turned the vision of his eyes on visible objects with a feeling of passion . . ."[4]

Symeon then asserts that those who marginalize the saints are prone to envy and irascibility just like Adam's son, Cain.[5] More to the point, Symeon indicates that holy men are being contradicted in his own time for pointing out the follies of those who are worldly minded, as well as being questioned for their experience of God's uncreated energies in the form of divine light.[6] As mentioned above, both the New Theologian and his mentor were treated with suspicion by their contemporaries, many of whom were no longer cherishing the inner life, having reduced the spiritual enterprise to the imposition and maintenance of external forms of devotion. Throughout his corpus, Symeon discloses that the monastic tradition is in danger of being misappropriated by proponents of a fanatic ritualism stressing the authority of abbots and the rhythms of corporate worship at the expense of the inner life, thus denying the central message of the gospel and the Orthodox tradition more generally: that deification can be experienced in the here and now by every person through practical asceticism (e.g., fasting and keeping vigil) and contemplation (e.g., a constant focus on Christ and reflection on the principles of his creation).[7]

Symeon thus expresses his outrage at the hypocritical attitude of those who "twist the whole of Scripture according to their own desires (2 Pet

<hr>

3. Maloney, "Introduction" to Symeon the New Theologian, *Discourses*, 14–19.

4. Symeon the New Theologian, *Discourses* 15.1, 193.

5. Symeon the New Theologian, *Discourses* 15.1, 193.

6. Symeon the New Theologian, *Discourses* 15.1–2, 193–94.

7. For a summary of Symeon's theological framework (including his understanding of contemplation) and its consistency with the earlier patristic tradition, Alfeyev, *St. Symeon the New Theologian and Orthodox Tradition*, 169–74.

3:3, 16) and corrupt themselves in their own passions."[8] He condemns such people for denying others freedom in the Spirit whilst daring to exploit the church as a pyramid of power, and for advocating a conformist attitude coupled with a foreign, intellectualist theology. Take, for instance, his allusion to his major antagonist, Stephen:

> Even though he reads their visible records thousands of times with his physical eyes, the record that has been committed to writing, yet I do not think that such a person will ever be able to contemplate things that are spiritual, immaterial, and full of light in a place that is material and in darkness.[9]

Symeon goes on to describe the mystical union effected between God and the human person through grace, on the one hand, and practical asceticism and contemplation, on the other.[10] The New Theologian's description stems from his own experiences, which he explains in *Discourses* 16 and 22.[11] The saint subsequently combines the themes of adoption, rebirth and intimate union with God—including the image of Christ as the True Vine and the disciples as his branches (John 15:1–17)—to identify the sanctified, spiritual family constituting the authentic church.[12] He goes on to distinguish this family from those "who have not been changed at all in action, knowledge and contemplation[,]" that is, who have neglected the inner life, whatever the reason may be.[13] We may infer that humility is another marker of this family via his ensuing criticism of those who are in positions of authority within the church yet neither engage in asceticism nor seek to repent.[14]

The church father brings *Discourse* 15 to a close by imploring his audience to repent and keep the commandments, that they might be deified in this life. He underscores how the paradisal mode can experienced as a foretaste within the human heart whilst urgently pleading, "Run, seek, knock, that the door of the kingdom of heaven may be opened to you (Matt 7:7; Luke 11:9) and you may enter within it and have it within you (Luke 17:21)."[15] The saint thus challenges us to interiorize the gospel, that

---

8. Symeon the New Theologian, *Discourses* 15.2, 194.

9. Symeon the New Theologian, *Discourses* 15.2, 195.

10. Symeon the New Theologian, *Discourses* 15.3, 195–96.

11. Symeon the New Theologian, *Discourses* 16 and 22, 198–203, 243–53.

12. Symeon the New Theologian, *Discourses* 15.3, 195–96.

13. Symeon the New Theologian, *Discourses* 15.4, 196.

14. Symeon the New Theologian, *Discourses* 15.4–5, 196–97.

15. Symeon the New Theologian, *Discourses* 15.5, 197.

we may overcome the defeatist attitude characteristic of the fallen world, reminding us that that the Lord will reward all who remain vigilant. In a masterful piece of exegesis, the theologian also underscores the natural relationship between asceticism and good works whilst depicting Christ at the universal judgment seat.[16]

Contrary to those who attempt to ossify tradition through dull ritualism, on the one hand, and armchair theology, on the other, Symeon contends that the gift of the Holy Spirit was never restricted to the first Christian generations. Rather, the Spirit has always been active in the lives of his saints, and no genuine ecclesial experience exists without his presence; he has always inspired, informed, and guided the church. Hence the significance of contemplation; it enlivens the psychosomatic makeup of the human person, rendering them more receptive to the divine light and subsequently enabling them to relate to their community who God is based on direct revelation. Dogma, therefore, is the canonical expression of a lifestyle centered on the rule of prayer and selfless conduct. Truly, Symeon demonstrates what it means to be a bearer of the Holy Spirit in his zeal to celebrate the egalitarian nature of God's gifts whilst at the same time respecting the hierarchical framework of the church.

16. Symeon the New Theologian, *Discourses* 15.5, 197.

14

St. Gregory Palamas on Theology and Science

WE ARE OFTEN FACED with the question of whether theology and science can coexist and interact peacefully. Granted, many scholars have outlined how distinctive features of the Western Christian traditions explain the emergence of modern science in Europe during the seventeenth century. It is no secret that the Roman Catholic and Protestant Churches helped motivate the development of modern science, gave social legitimation to its practice, provided presuppositions without which its emergence would not have been possible, and contributed to specific methods of enquiry distinctive of the field. Yet what about our own church's attitude towards science generally, rooted as it is in the common discernment of the Byzantine fathers. To be sure, formal study of the natural world in and of itself began in ancient Greece and continued throughout the Middle Ages, often being of formative value and personal interest to our patristic authorities.[1] For the purpose of our discussion, let us appeal to our father among the saints, Gregory Palamas, possibly the greatest theologian of the fourteenth century (most often cited for his formal articulation of God's essence and uncreated energies, and the latter's implications for the spiritual life).[2]

1. For a comprehensive, diachronic exploration of the subject, see Buxhoeveden et al., *Science and the Eastern Orthodox Church*; Lawson, *Science in the Ancient World* (complete details within the bibliography).

2. The essence/energies distinction has always been part of the Orthodox tradition,

Although Gregory's biography is beyond the scope of our topic, may it suffice to state that he proceeded through the classical *trivium* and *quadrivium* constituting Byzantine education until the age of twenty, thus becoming an expert in the works of Aristotle before embracing the monastic life.[3] This philosophical formation would come to the fore in the church father's *One Hundred and Fifty Chapters*, wherein Gregory suggests that reality ought to be considered from a variety of perspectives whilst underscoring the value of both science and theology. The saint affirms that the former discipline refers to the study of God and the destiny of the human being whilst the latter concerns the examination of the natural world. This distinction will be examined in due course. For the moment, it must be noted that the saint was compelled to compose the text to refute the intelligentsia of his time, which consisted of Western scholastics, on the one hand, and Byzantine humanists, on the other.[4]

By failing to take notice of the epistemological distinction outlined by Gregory, the scholastics presumed that theology was chiefly dependent upon philosophy, that it stemmed from rational deduction like any other discipline as opposed to the divine revelation granted to those who genuinely engage in practical asceticism and contemplation.[5] Interestingly, the humanists were likewise guilty of confusing science with theology. This was due to their penchant for Hellenism, which inspired Gregory to counter their mythological depiction of reality via the Stoic and Neo-Platonic doctrine of the "world soul." This was held to control the sensible world and be the source of the immaterial aspect of the human person rather than Christ, the Only Begotten Son and Word of God. Since the fathers rarely address matters that do not pose an immediate threat to the church, one can infer that many intellectuals of the fourteenth century had neo-pagan

---

safeguarding the fundamental truth that God totally transcends yet fully operates within creation. It became more clearly articulated by Gregory in his defence of the Athonite community's practice of hesychasm; that is, their retiring inward and repeated citation of the Jesus Prayer to transcend all sensible distractions, thereby achieving experiential knowledge of, and union with, God (to the extent that this possible for created beings). See Ware, *Orthodox Way*, 22–23, 123–26; Ware, "St. Nikodemos and the Philokalia," 28; Russell, *Gregory Palamas and the Making of Palamism in the Modern Age*, 32.

3. Meyendorff, *St. Gregory Palamas and Orthodox Spirituality*, 71–73.

4. Sinkewicz, "Introduction" to Gregory Palamas, *One Hundred and Fifty Chapters*, 1–49; Palmer et al., "Introductory Note" to Gregory Palamas, *Topics of Natural and Theological Science and on the Moral and Ascetic Life*, 290–92.

5. Costache, "Other Path in Science, Theology and Spirituality," 48.

propensities.[6] Gregory thus refutes the false perceptions of the scholastics from the viewpoint of theology. Conversely, he counters the misconceptions of the humanists through the lens of science.

The church father's mastery of science and theology is demonstrated in the first chapter, where he states that the beginning of the world is attested to by the Scriptures, in addition to the secular sciences, the arts, and different societal factors.[7] This indicates that Gregory allowed for the convergence of different fields of knowledge for the purpose of understanding the wider cosmos. The saint's fondness for science becomes even more apparent as he addresses topics pertaining to cosmology, geology, epistemology, and the mechanisms of human perception whilst appealing to Aristotle.[8] Indeed, he cites the Stagirite to refute the pagan doctrine of "world soul," mentioned above. For Gregory, the conventional sciences were able to sufficiently explain natural phenomena.[9] Nonetheless, within the first chapter, the saint suggests that the Scriptures ought to be of greater value for Christians: "we see none of the first writers on any subject whatever surpassing the account of the beginning of the world and of time, as Moses recorded it."[10] It should not be assumed that Gregory's theological viewpoint concerning creation excludes all others. The Scriptures are not superior to other forms of literature owing to their depiction of the world's formation. Rather, they are more significant for believers because they relate to and inform our relationship with God.

The church father explicitly distinguishes between secular (i.e., natural) and theological (i.e., divinely inspired) knowledge in the twentieth and twenty-first chapters. In the former, he describes the scientific discipline as facilitating the acquisition of knowledge through the observation of the visible realm. This knowledge, gathered through the senses and

6. Siniossoglou, *Radical Platonism in Byzantium*, 261.

7. Gregory Palamas, *One Hundred and Fifty Chapters* 1, 83.

8. Gregory Palamas, *One Hundred and Fifty Chapters* 1–19, 82–103.

9. "We know not only the phenomena of the moon but also those of the sun, both the solar eclipses and their nodes, the parallaxes of the other celestial planets and the distances separating them and the manifold configurations formed thereby, and the phenomena of the heavens in general. And further, the laws of nature and all its methods and arts, and in general all knowledge of anything collected from perception of particulars, we have gathered together from the senses and the imagination through the mind . . ." Gregory Palamas, *One Hundred and Fifty Chapters* 20, 103. Costache, "Other Path in Science, Theology and Spirituality," 49

10. Gregory Palamas, *One Hundred and Fifty Chapters* 1, 83.

subsequently represented and interpreted in the mind, cannot, however, "ever be called spiritual but rather natural, which does not attain the things of the Spirit."[11] Gregory therefore posits that our sensory perceptions need to be guided and informed by the Holy Spirit prior to undertaking any theological speculation. He continues with this line of reasoning in the subsequent chapter: "Where can we learn anything certain and free from deceit about God, about the world as a whole, about our own selves? Is it not from the teaching of the Spirit?"[12]

It must be highlighted that the church father does not suggest that the sciences do not matter, or that theology is the only discipline of interest to him since it is based on divine revelation. His general appreciation for science, displayed consistently throughout the previous chapters, obviously proves otherwise. Rather, Gregory asserts that the natural sciences, whilst benefiting humanity in several ways, do not contribute to the spiritual formation of Christians per se. The implication is that only direct communion with the Spirit through practical asceticism and contemplation can enable us to properly interpret the levels of reality concerning God and the inner life of the faithful: "For this teaching has taught us that God alone is true being, eternal being and immutable being, that he neither received being out of non-being nor returns to non-being, and that he is trihypostatic and omnipotent."[13]

In the twenty-ninth chapter, the saint levels the accusation made against the early church that Christians were unlearned, at the same time drawing a parallel to his own context, that is, his having been openly and repeatedly criticized together with his fellow Athonites by Barlaam the Calabrian, on the one hand, and Nikephoros Gregoras, on the other.[14] Gregory thus recapitulates his argument, insisting that scientific knowledge is irrelevant for those who solely desire spiritual formation. Rather, such people ought to examine themselves and humbly acknowledge their shortcomings: "For the mind that realizes its own weakness has discovered whence it might enter upon salvation and draw near to the light of knowledge and receive true wisdom which does not pass away with this age."[15]

---

11. Gregory Palamas, *One Hundred and Fifty Chapters* 20, 103.

12. Gregory Palamas, *One Hundred and Fifty Chapters* 21, 103.

13. Gregory Palamas, *One Hundred and Fifty Chapters* 21, 103.

14. Tatakis, *Christian Philosophy in the Patristic and Byzantine Tradition*, 157–59.

15. Gregory Palamas, *One Hundred and Fifty Chapters* 29, 113.

In summary, Gregory teaches us that theology and science can co-exist and interact peacefully provided that their individual competencies are properly delineated. The saint was among the first popular thinkers to convey the idea that different branches of learning are equipped with specific tools that enable their proponents to perceive different layers of reality. Considering his transdisciplinary approach, the saint also maintained that no single field of inquiry might enable humanity to interpret every layer since each has its own aim and axiomatic references. Gregory never denies the validity of scientific inquiry in his *Chapters* so long as it pertains to the natural world. The faithful can thus appeal to the saint to refute those who claim to be Orthodox yet display a fundamentalist attitude in wholly condemning the different branches of modern science. Moreover, he serves as an example to Christian scholars by reminding them that the study of theology requires a living relationship with God. Consistent with Macarius the Homilist and Maximus the Confessor, Gregory maintains that theology is experiential, not theoretical, at its core. Doctrine thus stems from prayer, asceticism, and regular partaking of the sacraments. Having nurtured the inner life and achieved a certain level of discernment, Orthodox academics will be able to cross disciplinary boundaries and forge holistic methodologies, facilitating projects that contribute to their wider communities' understanding of the sensible and intelligible realms.

15

St. Mitrophan the Martyr and the Boxer Rebellion

[Christians] love all men, and are persecuted by all. They are unknown, and yet they are condemned; they are put to death, and yet they give proof of new life. They are poor, and yet make many rich; they lack everything, and yet in everything they abound. They are dishonoured, and their dishonour becomes their glory; they are reviled, and yet are vindicated. They are abused, and they bless; they are insulted, and repay insult with honour. They do good, and are punished as evil-doers; and in their punishment they rejoice as finding new life therein.   *The Epistle to Diognetus* 5.11–16[1]

THE ABOVE PASSAGE IS from an eloquent defense of the Christian faith composed by an enigmatic author of the second century known only as "Mathetes." In short, the author is keen to emphasize how his faith community maintains its spiritual integrity despite the various hardships which it must endure at the hands of its pagan authorities. Mathetes suggests that the church's steadfastness is best demonstrated by its loving disposition towards its enemies. Owing to its moral earnestness—which has been directly inspired by the Triune God—the church is markedly different from the remainder of the world. And yet, as the body of Christ, it paradoxically serves as the true life of the fallen cosmos, much like the soul does with respect to the body. According to Mathetes, although the soul and the church are both unjustly despised by their respective environments for denying them illicit

---

1. *Epistle to Diognetus* 5.11–16, 64–65.

pleasures, they nonetheless mystically sustain them in their obedience to God.[2] This profound observation applies to the church in every epoch, every civilization. In what follows, I shall attempt to outline how the phenomenon of martyrdom extended to the Far East during the early modern era, paying close attention to the greatest paragon of the Orthodox faith in this region, that is, our righteous father Mitrophan Chi Sung, the first indigenous Chinese presbyter and holy martyr of the Boxer Rebellion.

The Chinese were initially exposed to aspects of the gospel by schismatic groups—predominantly East Assyrians and Nestorians—during Late Antiquity. For this reason, it is no surprise that the Christian faith did not take root in China as it did throughout Asia Minor and the European Continent, where Orthodoxy had for the most part triumphed during the first millennium. The schismatic groups in Asia were in fact persecuted during the ninth century by the Chinese authorities and were eventually extinguished in the High Middle Ages, specifically during the latter's fierce conflicts with the Mongols (among whom the Nestorians had enjoyed great success). The material evidence pertaining to these communities was for the most part destroyed by the Buddhist and pagan Chinese authorities, on the one hand, and later Roman Catholic missionaries, on the other.[3]

The Orthodox Christian faith was introduced to China in the early modern period. The first Orthodox Christians known to have entered the Oriental superpower were Russians that adhered to the Greek tradition, and who served in the ranks of the Western Army of the Mongols. When the Western Army returned to China in 1240, the Greek Orthodox Russians established a small church whose whereabouts have sadly been forgotten. Around this time, goldsmiths from Russia were invited to the Chinese imperial court to fashion what is known as the "Elephant's Tooth Throne." These were likely men of faith, although we are not certain how long they stayed in China or what social influence they had. Orthodoxy reappears in the historical records of China in 1671, when a church dedicated to the resurrection was constructed in the northeastern province, Yakela. This territory had long been fought over by the Russians and the Chinese and was to prove instrumental in God's plan for the Far East.[4]

2. *Epistle to Diognetus* 6, 66–68.

3. Baker, "Wise Men from the East," 49–51; McGuckin, "China, Autonomous Orthodox Church of," 112; Yaokum and Chen, "Beyond the Great Wall," 3.

4. Baker, "Wise Men from the East," 52.

Between 1681 and 1685, the Chinese authorities captured no less than ninety-nine Russian Orthodox Christians in the territorial dispute. At least forty-four of these were Cossacks, members of one the self-governing, soldiering communities that had originated in the steppes of Eastern Europe, in particular the Dnieper, otherwise known as the "Wild Field." They were taken from a fort at Albazin along the Amur River, which forms the border between the Russian Far East and Northern China. More precisely, the men were brought to the imperial capital, Beijing, where they were soon pardoned by the Kangxi Emperor of the Qing Dynasty. Many of them took Chinese wives whilst preserving their Christian faith, also serving as the emperor's bodyguards.[5] It should be noted that our Most Holy Lady Theotokos displayed great mercy to the people of Albazin during these years of arduous conflict, regularly defending them against raids and sieges, particularly through her wonderworking icon, "The Word Made Flesh." This icon had been brought to the region by a certain Elder Hermogenes from the Monastery of the Holy Trinity at Kirensk in Irkutsk Oblast.[6]

Providentially, a priest happened to be among the captives-turned-citizens, that is, Father Maxime Leontiev, who established and served at Beijing's first Orthodox church. The structure was gifted to the faith community by the Kangxi Emperor when it elected to stay after the armistice declared by the latter. Interestingly, the building had hitherto functioned as a pagan temple dedicated to the Chinese god of war, Guandi.[7] It now served the Prince of Peace, that is, our Lord Jesus Christ (Isa 9:6). Following the ancient Orthodox custom, the temple was reconsecrated as a church dedicated to Holy Wisdom with the blessing of the Holy Metropolitan Ignatius of Tobolsk. It was later re-founded as the Church of the Holy Dormition and continued to be served by Fr. Maxime who—in a manner attesting to the favorable relations between Beijing and the budding Russian diaspora—was granted the title of "Imperial Official of the Seventh Rank" by the emperor. The presbyter was also encouraged to proclaim the good news of salvation to the wider society by his Metropolitan, and an additional church was soon constructed and dedicated to St. Nicholas.[8]

5. Baker, "Wise Men from the East," 52; McGuckin, "China, Autonomous Orthodox Church of," 112; Yaokum and Chen, "Beyond the Great Wall," 3–4.

6. Orthodox Church in America, "Icon of the Mother of God, 'Albazin" or "Word Was Made Flesh," lines 30–38.

7. Baker, "Wise Men from the East," 52; McGuckin, "China, Autonomous Orthodox Church of," 112; Yaokum and Chen, "Beyond the Great Wall," 4.

8. Baker, "Wise Men from the East," 52; McGuckin, "China, Autonomous Orthodox

Following Fr. Maxime's repose in 1712, Father Hilarion Lezhaisky, an archimandrite, was sent by the Russian Patriarchate to tend the small flock in Beijing. Fr. Hilarion's mission commenced in 1715 and was more formal since it was the result of a peace treaty between Tsar Peter the Great and the abovementioned Chinese ruler. The mission itself features in official ecclesiastical and imperial records after 1727. In short, its chief purpose was to serve the Russian diplomatic staff that visited and resided in China. Interestingly, the faith community was referred to as "Greek Orthodox" by the Chinese, who thereby acknowledged its Byzantine origins. Whilst another treaty concerning the rights of the Orthodox Church allowed for the residence of only four priests and six students in Beijing, the mission continued to expand, especially among the descendants of the seventeenth-century prisoners and the increasing number of tradesmen and merchants arriving from Russia. Thus, another church was opened in 1732 and, almost a century and a half later, there were approximately five hundred Orthodox Christians residing in Beijing. It is noteworthy that the archimandrites who led the mission during this time also represented the Tsar and were therefore required to actively engage in treaty negotiations and other forms of political diplomacy.[9]

The Russian mission eventually introduced Chinese literary classics into Europe while strengthening ties between its native and adoptive homelands at the political level. Subsequently, during the nineteenth century, following the change of the Russian ecclesiastical legation, the mission began to reach the indigenous Chinese population. This largely owed to the pastoral care and cultural sensitivity of Fathers Hyacinth Bichurin and Palladii, both of whom managed to master the Chinese language and translate Orthodox literature for the wider populace. Not only did they produce the first ever copy of the New Testament in the Chinese language, but they also set up multiple catechetical centers in Beijing and elsewhere. They also allowed services to be partly held in the native language so that, by 1871, ten to forty Chinese people were embracing Orthodoxy annually.[10]

Such blessed work continued under Fr. Palladii's successor, Archimandrite Innocent (later elevated to the office of Metropolitan), so that there were

---

Church of," 112; Yaokum and Chen, "Beyond the Great Wall," 4.

9. Baker, "Wise Men from the East," 52–53; McGuckin, "China, Autonomous Orthodox Church of," 112–13.

10. Baker, "Wise Men from the East," 53; McGuckin, "China, Autonomous Orthodox Church of," 112–13.

daily Orthodox services in Chinese by 1897. This was in addition to various pastoral programs, including almsgiving. The mission also extended to the surrounding rural communities.[11] Merely a year or two later, however, the mission was to encounter a devastating challenge in the form of a populist and nationalistic movement directed against foreigners and their growing social influence, chiefly those who claimed to be Christian.

Mitrophan was born "Chi Sung" on the 10th of December, 1855, to a family associated with the Russian Orthodox mission in Beijing. We know of his life and martyrdom from Archimandrite Innocent, as well as another priest of equal rank by the name of Abraham. In short, Mitrophan lost his father as a child and was subsequently raised by his mother, Marina, and grandmother, Ekaterina. By all accounts, he was shy and modest, and devoted to the mission from a young age. His virtue was such that he would bare the greatest of insults without ever attempting to justify himself. Mitrophan was also very generous throughout his life, so that many took advantage of him. He was invited to be ordained many times by the mission's authorities but often refused on account of his humility. According to Fathers Innocent and Abraham, Mitrophan would assert that he could not accept the prestigious rank since he lacked the required virtues and charisms.[12] Indeed, he is remembered by contemporary Orthodox in Shanghai to have said, "I am just a simple, uneducated man, how can I become a priest? How can I stand before the fearful altar of God?"[13] Nevertheless, in 1880 he consented to the wishes of both the clergy and laity among his community. At the behest of the industrious missionary, Archimandrite Flavian, he went to the celebrated Russian bishop of Tokyo, St. Nikolai of Japan, to be baptized and ordained. The renowned church father and missionary happened to be visiting China at the time. Chi Sung thus became the first native Chinese priest of the Orthodox Church and received the name "Mitrophan" before returning home.[14]

It is noteworthy that Mitrophan was married to an Orthodox woman from the mission's Li family named "Tatiana." They had three sons: Isaiah, Serge, and John. Isaiah served in the military and was married to a fellow

---

11. Baker, "Wise Men from the East," 53.

12. Johnson, *Searching for Jesus on the Silk Road*, 185–90, esp., 187; Baker, *History of the Orthodox Church in China, Korea, and Japan*, 144.

13. Yaokum and Chen, "Beyond the Great Wall," 11.

14. Johnson, *Searching for Jesus on the Silk Road*, 185; Yaokum and Chen, "Beyond the Great Wall," 11.

Chinese Orthodox of the Beijing mission whose Christian name was "Mary." Serge followed in his father's footsteps and became an archpriest. John was much younger than his brothers and perhaps the most favored by the Lord, since he received the crown of martyrdom at the tender age of eight.[15]

For the fifteen years following his ordination, Mitrophan worked tirelessly for the mission under Fr. Flavian, translating and proofreading liturgical books. Tragically, he was looked down upon by many of his contemporaries—both Chinese and Russian Orthodox—who criticized his ostensibly poor theological education and chanting skills. Fathers Innocent and Abraham nonetheless celebrated his work, as well as his ability to endure contempt and harm from people everywhere.[16] True to his temperament and faithful to the Lord's exhortations, Mitrophan continued to preach, serve, and translate peacefully. He was eventually struck with a mental illness, which current Orthodox from Shanghai speculate was an affliction related to memory. He therefore retired from the mission to a place nearby, receiving half of his former salary as his pension.[17]

At the beginning of the twentieth century, China was experiencing several calamities, including poverty, natural disasters, and foreign aggression in and around its territories. This led to social unrest in the north especially, which had a reputation for its religious sects and martial societies. A revolt was therefore initiated by the self-proclaimed *Yihetuan*, that is, "Militia United in Righteousness," which harbored resentment to all foreign powers owing to the socio-economic factors mentioned above, as well as pagan superstition and cultural and legal disputes on the local level with the Catholic and Protestant denominations. The uprising came to be sponsored by the last ruler of the Qing Dynasty, Empress Dowager Cixi, who declared war with the British Empire, Russia, Japan, France, Germany, the United States, Italy, and the Dual Monarchy of Austria-Hungary. Subsequently, the rebellion was not against the established government or leader of China, but the tradesmen and missionaries which had settled in the land. The uprising led to a large-scale conflict, which in turn resulted in one hundred thousand civilian and military deaths, among them

---

15. Johnson, *Searching for Jesus on the Silk Road*, 185, 188; Baker, *History of the Orthodox Church in China, Korea, and Japan*, 144–45.

16. Johnson, *Searching for Jesus on the Silk Road*, 187.

17. Johnson, *Searching for Jesus on the Silk Road*, 187; Yaokum and Chen, "Beyond the Great Wall," 11; Baker, *History of the Orthodox Church in China, Korea, and Japan*, 145.

countless Orthodox, Roman Catholics, and Protestants of different ethnic backgrounds, in addition to indigenous Chinese.[18]

The *Yihetuan* movement came to be known in English as the "Boxer Rebellion" because many of those who comprised it practiced martial arts, otherwise referred to in this period by Westerners as "Chinese Boxing." Yet the *Yihetuan* were not concerned with martial arts per se. Rather, they constituted a religious cult since they performed a series of rituals in which they sought to be taken over by one of the pagan gods in the Chinese pantheon (i.e., the demons) that they might become immune to Western types of weaponry. They thus entered trances in which they violently wielded swords and spears whilst dancing wildly. The rituals originated from peasants in the Yellow River floodplain and were transmitted from village to village in Northern China, resulting in what may be considered mass shamanism. This was literal—not simply ideological—possession on the part of hundreds of thousands of people.[19] Archimandrites Innocent and Abraham described the chilling days in which the Orthodox, Catholics, and Protestants were hunted down in Beijing, the most significant of which was June 10, 1900. In brief, leaflets were distributed in the streets on this day demanding the execution of Christians and anyone who attempted to hide or defend them. The Boxers ran throughout Beijing with torches, laying waste to Christian houses and seizing their occupants. Many Orthodox, Catholics, and Protestants were forced to deny our Lord by offering incense before the pagan Chinese idols. Some, however, confessed the Savior, and were in turn subjected to being torn open, decapitated, or burnt alive. The killings continued the next day, when the Christians were brought to the temples of the Boxers to be interrogated. Those that remained faithful to the Lord were burnt at the stake.[20]

The destruction spread to the cities of Kalgan and Tung-Tingan.[21] There is an obvious parallel here between the experience of the first Orthodox in China and our common forebears in the Roman Empire. Whilst the violent suppression of Orthodoxy was sporadic until the accession of St. Constantine the Great, countless followers of the Son and Word of God

18. Baker, *History of the Orthodox Church in China, Korea, and Japan*, 135–44; Esherick, *Origins of the Boxer Uprising*, 167–205; "Beyond the Great Wall," 11 n. 2.

19. Esherick, *Origins of the Boxer Uprising*, xiii–iv, 206–40.

20. Johnson, *Searching for Jesus on the Silk Road*, 186.

21. Baker, *History of the Orthodox Church in China, Korea, and Japan*, 143; Baker, "Wise Men from the East," 53–54.

were unjustly executed over the first four centuries. Again, this was due to social resentment and pagan superstition sanctioned by the state. The types of murder were often the same as those that took place in China during the awful uprising, as were the forms of torture aimed at compelling denial of our Savior. Indeed, the offering of incense to the pagan gods was first established by the Romans as a means of acquittal.[22] Moreover, the spiritual fortitude described in the early martyr acts is identical to that attributed to the Chinese faithful by Fathers Innocent and Abraham. Take, for instance, Paul Wang, the catechist who openly prayed as he was being executed, and Ia Wang, the schoolteacher who experienced martyrdom twice: first, by being slashed by swords and buried alive; next, after being bravely rescued by a non-Christian attendant, through torture. There were also many descendants of the Albazinians who—in imitation of St. Stephen the Protomartyr—fearlessly confessed our Lord while imploring him to forgive their executioners. Clement Kui Lin, Anna Chui, and the brothers Matthew Chai and Witt Tsuang are among those still remembered by name.[23]

Earlier, on the evening of June 1, the Boxers had set the central site of the Beijing mission on fire. This included the library, whose resources had been prepared with much love and toil.[24] Several Orthodox therefore gathered and sought refuge at Mitrophan's house, among them those who had earlier mocked the saint. Mitrophan accepted them all graciously and encouraged those that were falling into despair by reminding them of the inevitable tribulations which all Christians must face. Movingly, he would venture out with courage to the burnt remains of the mission numerous times daily, to gaze at the cinders of his church and salvage what he could. On June 10, at about 10 p.m., Boxers surrounded his house accompanied by state soldiers, many of whom were Muslim. Seventy people had remained inside—mostly women and children, together with Mitrophan—all of whom were martyred. Ironically, the physically strongest members were the ones that chose to flee.[25]

Mitrophan humbly faced the Boxers while sitting in his yard. He refused to deny his faith for their misguided sense of patriotism, recognizing

---

22. Dunstan, *Ancient Rome*, 35; Rhee, *Early Christian Literature*, 88–89.

23. Johnson, *Searching for Jesus on the Silk Road*, 186–87; Baker, *History of the Orthodox Church in China, Korea, and Japan*, 148–51.

24. McGuckin, "China, Autonomous Orthodox Church of," 113.

25. Johnson, *Searching for Jesus on the Silk Road*, 187–88; Baker, *History of the Orthodox Church in China, Korea, and Japan*, 144–47.

the heavenly kingdom as his true and lasting abode. He viewed Orthodoxy as the sole faith which unites all people. The Boxers thus seized him and proceeded to stab his chest so savagely that it appeared like a beehive. He then fell under a date tree and gave up his soul to Lord.[26] The degree of *Christomimesis* on the part of Mitrophan is remarkable. The church father attempted to save and console his flock even though it had rejected him, knowing full well that this act of mercy would cost him his life. He was even willing to risk the lives of his wife and children for the sake of his enemies. It is also striking that he died under a tree. According to the sixth century Italian poet, Arator, the tree that is our Lord's Cross—the image of perfect obedience to the will of God the Father—removed the sin and death that entered the world through the Tree of Knowledge of Good and Evil—the most powerful symbol of humanity's disobedience. The tree on which our Lord was humiliated for our sakes also destroyed Satan.[27] We can therefore see that Mitrophan providentially fell under a tree to show us that he participated in our Lord's final victory over evil. He completely conformed to and attained Christ, the Tree of Life who joins heaven and earth in his very person. He partook of the same cup out of perfect love for God and neighbor (Matt 20:22-23).

Returning to Mitrophan's family, Tatiana had managed to escape with Mary's help, but on the next morning was captured and beheaded with other Orthodox faithful. Isaiah—who was known as a Christian among his fellow soldiers—had already been beheaded on June 7 on the main street near the Ping-tse-Min gates. On June 8, Mary returned to the house of her father-in-law. She refused to leave the place where she had been born owing to the fact that it was close to the Church of the Mother of God, her glorious patron. Mary was killed with her father-in-law two days later.[28]

It must be emphasized that Mitrophan could have sought refuge at the Russian embassy, while Mary had been given the chance to escape with Serge.[29] The good shepherd instead chose to remain with his sheep that it might not scatter. His daughter-in-law and disciple valiantly imitated his example. The same is true for his little boy, John, whose nose,

26. Johnson, *Searching for Jesus on the Silk Road*, 188; Baker, *History of the Orthodox Church in China, Korea, and Japan*, 146.

27. Arator, *Arator's On the Acts of the Apostles* 1, 30.

28. Johnson, *Searching for Jesus on the Silk Road*, 188; Baker, *History of the Orthodox Church in China, Korea, and Japan*, 146–48.

29. Yaokum and Chen, "Beyond the Great Wall," 11–12.

ears, and toes were chopped off by the Boxers. John's shoulders and legs were also pierced three inches deep. Owing to God's grace, however, the child felt no pain and dispassionately endured the mocking and callous treatment of his neighbors. The latter would not even offer him something to drink upon request. Although Mary tried to hide him in an outhouse prior to her own martyrdom, the boy was apprehended once more and taken to be executed. He showed no signs of fear.[30]

The tragic events of the Boxer Rebellion gave our church numerous martyrs: two hundred and twenty-two by one estimate, four hundred by another.[31] The Boxer Rebellion was, in fact, an ominous sign of the persecution and heartache that the church was to experience soon after under the communists in Russia and what was to become the Soviet Union. However, it also functioned a prelude to the period of greatest expansion of Orthodoxy throughout China in a manner consistent with the famous assertion of the second century apologist, Tertullian, that the blood of the martyrs constitutes the seed from which the church grows.[32] Following the violent suppression of the rebellion by the Western powers, the church managed to flourish again in China so that by 1914 there were at least thirty-two Orthodox mission centers scattered throughout the nation comprised of five to six thousand clergymen and laypeople. The centers included monasteries, schools, and chapels. More Russian Orthodox eventually fled to China owing the Bolshevik Revolution of 1917, thereby enriching the Orthodox community which, by the 1940s, extended from Beijing to Wuhan, Harbin, Henan, Hubei, Shanghai, Xinjiang, and Manchuria.[33]

Largely due to Russia's neutral position with respect to China throughout most of World War II, the Orthodox Church managed to survive and even flourish in the Far East until the early 1950s. In 1950 specifically, the Metropolitan of Moscow consecrated the first ever indigenous Chinese hierarch, His Grace Bishop Symeon (born "Du Run-chen"), a survivor of the Boxer Rebellion. Bishop Symeon was given authority over Tianjin then Shanghai, where he served as an industrious pastor and apostle. In 1955/1956, the Russian Patriarchate granted semi-autonomous status to

---

30. Johnson, *Searching for Jesus on the Silk Road*, 188–89; Baker, *History of the Orthodox Church in China, Korea, and Japan*, 147–48.

31. McGuckin, "China, Autonomous Orthodox Church of," 113; Baker, "Wise Men from the East," 54.

32. Tertullian, *Apology* 50, 55.

33. McGuckin, "China, Autonomous Orthodox Church of," 113; Baker, "Wise Men from the East," 54.

the Orthodox Church in China, that it might continue to prosper unaffected by the communist authorities at the center of the Soviet Union. During this time, there were probably more than one hundred thousand communicants, two hundred presbyters, and sixty parishes in Northern China, in addition to two monasteries and a seminary. There were another two hundred thousand Orthodox Christians and one hundred and fifty parishes throughout the remainder of the country.[34]

The expansion described above underscores the even greater tragedy which the Chinese Orthodox Church experienced in 1966 with the Cultural Revolution initiated by Mao Zedong. This specific uprising attempted to preserve the recently introduced Chinese form of communism by purging society of all remnants of its agelong traditions, on the one hand, and capitalism, on the other. The churches throughout the nation were closed, desecrated, or destroyed, while all clergy and congregations were punished in some way. A great number of Christians were once again killed by the crowds.[35] Bishop Symeon was spared from witnessing this senseless destruction on the eve of the revolution, having reposed on account of ill health made worse by poverty.[36]

Since the Cultural Revolution of 1966, the Chinese communist state has refused to re-acknowledge and legally sanction Orthodoxy. Nevertheless, a heroic remnant of the church struggles to preserve the faith whilst celebrating and imitating the example of Mitrophan and the New Chinese Martyrs. Orthodox parishes can still be found in Beijing and certain parts of northeastern China, in addition to Shanghai, the Guangdong Province, Hong Kong, and Taiwan. The Russian Orthodox Church of Sts. Peter and Paul resumed services in Hong Kong a little more than a decade ago.[37] Moreover, in 1996, the Holy and Great Synod of the Ecumenical Patriarchate founded the Metropolitanate of Hong Kong and Southeast Asia. The jurisdiction of the Metropolitanate extends to areas of China, Taiwan, Macao, the Philippines, Vietnam, Cambodia, Laos, Thailand, Myanmar, and Mongolia.[38]

34. Baker, "Wise Men from the East," 54–55; Yaokum and Chen, "Beyond the Great Wall," 5–6.

35. Baker, *History of the Orthodox Church in China, Korea, and Japan*, 209–14; Baker, "Wise Men from the East," 55; Yaokum and Chen, "Beyond the Great Wall," 6–7.

36. Baker, *History of the Orthodox Church in China, Korea, and Japan*, 211; Yaokum and Chen, "Beyond the Great Wall," 6.

37. McGuckin, "China, Autonomous Orthodox Church of," 113–14.

38. "About Us," lines 1–25.

The experience of the Orthodox Church in China demonstrates how our Lord was true to his word when he said that his gospel would be proclaimed "in all the world as a witness to all the nations . . ." (Matt 24:14). Much like their forebears in Africa, Asia Minor, Egypt, Syria, and the European continent, the Chinese Orthodox were destined to experience the phenomenon of martyrdom, the first instance of which was due to populism, the second, socialism. Both cases are highly relevant to our times, in which the wider church must exercise altruistic compassion whilst navigating between the dangerous extremes of the far right and the far left. As concerns Mitrophan and the New Martyrs specifically, we recognize that they did not belong to this world and that the Lord chose them out of the world—hence why the world hated them. Indeed, the Lord revealed himself through them (John 15:18–25). They perfectly conformed to Christ in displaying love for their enemies even to the point of death. Subsequently, they were persecuted just as Christ was, remembering his exhortation: "be of good cheer, I have overcome the world" (John 16:33 NKJV). May we have the loving intercessions of the New Chinese Martyrs and let us imitate especially the meekness and profound courage of Mitrophan.

Bibliography

"About Us." Ecumenical Patriarchate Orthodox Metropolitanate of Hong Kong and Southeast Asia. https://www.omhksea.org/about.

Acta Proconsularia Sancti Cypriani. In *The Acts of the Christian Martyrs*, edited and translated by Herbert Musurillo, 168–75. Oxford: Clarendon, 1972.

The Acts of Peter. In *The Apocryphal Acts of Paul, Peter, John, Andrew and Thomas*, translated by Bernhard Pick, 50–122. Chicago: Open Court, 1909.

Adomnán of Iona. *Adomnán's Life of Columba.* Edited and translated by Alan Orr Anderson and Marjorie Ogilvie Anderson. London: Thomas Nelson and Sons, 1961.

———. *The Illustrated Life of Columba.* Translated by John Gregory. Prologue by John Marsden. Illustrations by Geoff Green. Edinburgh: Floris, 1995.

———. *Life of St Columba.* Translated by Richard Sharpe. London: Penguin. eBook edition.

Alexander, Dominic. *Saints and Animals in the Middle Ages.* Woodbridge, Suffolk, UK: Boydell, 2008.

Alfeyev, Hilarion. *St. Symeon the New Theologian and Orthodox Tradition.* Oxford: Oxford University Press, 2000.

Allen, Pauline. "Life and Times of Maximus the Confessor." In *The Oxford Handbook of Maximus the Confessor*, edited by Pauline Allen et al., 3–18. Oxford: Oxford University Press, 2015.

Allen, Pauline and Bronwen Neil, eds. *The Life of Maximus the Confessor, Recension 3.* Translated by Bronwen Neil and Pauline Allen. Early Christian Studies 6. Strathfield, New South Wales, Australia: St. Pauls, 2003.

———. *Maximus the Confessor and His Companions: Documents from Exile.* Translated by Bronwen Neil and Pauline Allen. Oxford: Oxford University Press, 2002.

Ambrose of Milan. *De officiis.* In *De officiis, Volume 1: Introduction, Text, and Translation*, edited and translated by Ivor J. Davidson. Oxford: Oxford University Press, 2001.

———. *Exposition of the Christian* Faith. In *Ambrose: Select Works and Letters*, translated by H. De Romestin et al., 201–314. Nicene and Post-Nicene Fathers, Ser. 2, Vol. 10. Edited by Philip Schaff et al. Peabody, MA: Hendrickson, 1995.

Andrew of Crete. *The Great Canon*. In *The Great Canon of Saint Andrew of Crete and The Life of Saint Mary of Egypt*, edited and translated by Mother Thekla et al., 46–98. N.p.: Finnian, 2013.

———. *Magnus Canon*. In *Patrologia cursus completes: Series greaca*, vol. 97, edited by Jacques-Paul Migne, 1329–85. Paris: Migne, 1865.

The Anonymous History of Abbot Ceolfrith. In *The Age of Bede*, translated by J. F. Webb, edited by D. H. Farmer, 344–65. London: Penguin. eBook edition.

Apophthegmata Patrum (Collectio Graeca alphabetica). In *Patrologia cursus completes: Series greaca*, vol. 65, edited by Jacques-Paul Migne, 71–440. Paris: Migne, 1864.

Apophthegmata Patrum, Collectio Graeca systematica. In *Les Apophtegmes des Pères, collection systématique 1–3*. Edited and translated by Jean-Claude Guy. Sources Chrétiennes 387, 474, 498. Paris: Les Éditions du Cerf, 1993, 2003, 2005.

Aquino, Frederick D. "The *Philokalia* and Regulative Virtue Epistemology: A Look at Maximus the Confessor." In *The Philokalia: A Classic Text of Orthodox Spirituality*, edited by Brock Bingaman et al., 240–51. Oxford: Oxford University Press, 2012.

Arator. *Arator's On the Acts of the Apostles*. Edited by Richard J. Schrader. Translated by Joseph L. Roberts and John F. Makowski. Classics in Religious Studies 6. Atlanta: Scholars, 1987.

Athanasius of Alexandria. *The Life of Antony: The Coptic Life and The Greek Life*. Translated by Tim Vivian et al. Cistercian Studies Series 202. Michigan: Cistercian, 2003.

———. *The Life of Antony and The Letter to Marcellinus*. Translated by Robert C. Gregg. Classics of Western Spirituality. Mahwah, NJ: Paulist, 1980.

———. *On the Incarnation*. Edited and translated by a Religious of C.S.M.V. Crestwood, NY: St Vladimir's Seminary Press, 1993.

Augustine of Hippo. *Augustin: Anti-Pelagian Writings*. Translated by Peter Holmes, Robert et al. Nicene and Post-Nicene Fathers, Ser. 1, Vol. 5. Edited by Philip Schaff. Peabody, MA: Hendrickson, 1995.

———. *Augustine's Commentary on Galatians*. Edited and translated by Eric Plumer. Oxford: Oxford University Press, 2003.

———. *Confessions*. Translated by Henry Chadwick. Oxford: Oxford University Press, 1991.

———. *Confessions*. Translated by R. S. Pine-Coffin. London: Penguin, 1961.

———. *Select Letters*. Translated by James Houston Baxter. Loeb Classical Library 239. London: William Heinemann, 1930.

Baghos, Chris. "The Apologetic and Literary Value of the Acts of Justin." *Phronema* 34:1 (2019) 25–54.

Baghos, Mario. "Hellenistic Globalisation and the Metanarrative of the Logos." *Thinking Diversely: Hellenism and the Challenge of Globalisation, A Special Edition of Modern Greek Studies, Australia and New Zealand: A Journal for Greek Letters* (2012) 23–37.

Baker, Kevin. *A History of the Orthodox Church in China, Korea, and Japan*. Lewiston, NY: Edwin Mellen, 2006.

———. "Wise Men from the East: The Influence of Eastern Christianity in China, 635–1986." *Phronema* 8 (1993) 49–56.

Barnard, L. W. *Justin Martyr: His Life and Thought*. London: Cambridge University Press, 1967.

Barsanuphius of Gaza and John the Prophet. *Letters, Volume 2.* Translated by John Chryssavgis. Fathers of the Church 114. Washington, DC: Catholic University of America Press, 2007.

Basil the Great. *To Ambrose, Bishop of Milan.* In *Letters, Volume II (186–368),* translated by Agnes Clare Way, 42–45. Fathers of the Church 28. Washington, DC: Catholic University of America Press, 1955.

Baur, Chrysostomus. *John Chrysostom and His Time,* vol. 1: *Antioch.* Translated by M. Gonzaga. Westminster, MD: Newman, 1959.

Bedas metrische Vita sankti Cuthberti. Edited by Werner Jaager. Leipzig: Mayer and Müller, 1935.

Bede the Venerable. *A History of the English Church and People.* Translated by Leo Sherley-Price. Harmondsworth, Middlesex, UK: Penguin, 1955.

———. *Lives of the Abbots of Wearmouth and Jarrow.* In *The Age of Bede,* translated by J. F. Webb, ed. D. H. Farmer, 304–65. London: Penguin. eBook edition.

———. *Vita Sancti Cuthberti.* In *Two Lives of Saint Cuthbert.* Edited and translated by Bertram Colgrave. Cambridge, UK: Cambridge University Press, 1940.

Bequette, John P. "Sulpicius Severus' *Life of Saint Martin*: The Saint and His Biographer as Agents of Cultural Transformation." *Logos* 13:2 (2010) 56–78.

Blowers, Paul M. "Gentiles of the Soul: Maximus the Confessor on the Substructure and Transformation of Human Passions." *Journal of Early Christian Studies* 4.1 (1996) 57–85.

The Book of Kells: Forty-Eight Pages and Details in Color from The Manuscript in Trinity College, Dublin. Selected and Introduced by Peter Brown. New York: Alfred A. Knopf, 1980.

The Book of the Elders: Sayings of the Desert Fathers, The Systematic Collection. Translated by John Wortley. Collegeville, MN: Liturgical, 2012.

Bosivert, Mathieu. "Origins: Comparative Perspectives." In *Encyclopedia of Monasticism,* edited by William M. Johnston et al., 959–68. London: Routledge, 2000.

Brendaniana: St. Brendan the Voyager in Story and Legend. Edited and translated by Denis O'Donghue. Dublin: Browne and Nolan, 1895.

Brown, Michelle P. "Bede's Life in Context." In *The Cambridge Companion to Bede,* edited by Scott DeGregorio, 3–24. Cambridge, UK: Cambridge University Press, 2010.

Buxhoeveden, Daniel, and Gayle Woloschak, eds. *Science and the Eastern Orthodox Church.* London: Routledge, 2016.

Chadwick, Henry. *The Early Church.* The Penguin History of the Church 1. London: Penguin, 1993.

Clancy, Finbarr G. "Imitating the Mysteries That You Celebrate: Martyrdom and Eucharist in the Early Patristic Period." In *The Great Persecution: The Proceedings of the Fifth Patristic Conference, Maynooth, 2003,* edited by D. Vincent Twomey et al., 106–40. Dublin: Four Courts, 2009.

Clarkson, Tim. *Columba.* Edinburgh: Birlinn, 2012. eBook edition.

Costache, Doru. "The Other Path in Science, Theology and Spirituality: Pondering a Fourteenth Century Byzantine Model." *Transdisciplinary Studies* 1 (2011) 39–54.

Cutrer, Meredith D. "Early Irish *Peregrinatio* as Salvation History." In *Prophecy, Fate and Memory in the Early and Medieval Celtic World,* edited by Jonathan M. Wooding et al., 76–91. Sydney Series in Celtic Studies 18. Sydney University Press, 2020.

Cyprian of Carthage. *Cyprian to the People Abiding in Thibaris*. In *Letters 1–81*, translated Rose Bernard Donna, 162–71. Fathers of the Church 51. Washington, DC: Catholic University of America Press, 1981.

Cyril of Alexandria. *Commentary on Isaiah*. In *Cyril of Alexandria*, translated by Norman Russell, 70–95. London: Routledge, 2000.

———. *Cyril's Letter to the Monks of Egypt*. In *St. Cyril of Alexandria and the Christological Controversy*, translated by John A. McGuckin, 245–61. Supplements to Vigiliae Christianae 23. Leiden: Brill, 1994.

Dal Toso, Giampietro. "Proairesis." In *The Brill Dictionary of St Gregory of Nyssa*, edited by Lucas Francisco Mateo-Seco et al., translated by Seth Cherney, 647–49. Leiden: Brill, 2013.

The Desert Fathers: Sayings of the Early Christian Monks. Translated by Benedicta Ward. London: Penguin, 2003.

The Divine Liturgy of Our Father Among the Saints John Chrysostom. Edited and translated by the Greek Orthodox Archdiocese of Australia Committee on the Translation of Liturgical Texts. Sydney: St Andrew's Orthodox Press, 2005.

Dunn, Marilyn. *The Emergence of Monasticism: From the Desert Fathers to the Early Middle Ages*. Carlton, Victoria, Australia: Blackwell Publishing, 2000.

Dunstan, William E. *Ancient Rome*. Plymouth, UK: Rowman and Littlefield Publishers, 2011.

The Earliest Life of Gregory the Great by an Anonymous Monk of Whitby. Edited and translated by Bertram Colgrave. Cambridge, UK: Cambridge University Press, 1968.

The Epistle to Diognetus. Translated by L. B. Radford. London: Society for Promoting Christian Knowledge, 1908.

Esherick, Joseph W. *The Origins of the Boxer Uprising*. University of California Press, 1987.

Eusebius of Caesarea. *Ecclesiastical History, Volume I: Books 1–5*. Translated by Kirsopp Lake. Loeb Classical Library 153. Cambridge, MA: Harvard University Press, 1926.

———. *Ecclesiastical History, Volume II: Books 6–10*. Translated by J. E. L. Oulton, Loeb Classical Library 265. Cambridge, MA: Harvard University Press, 1932.

Felix. *Vita Sancti Guthlaci*. In *Felix's Life of Saint Guthlac*. Edited and translated by Bertram Colgrave. Cambridge, UK: Cambridge University Press, 1956.

Gildas the Wise. *The Ruin of Britain*. In *Gildas: The Ruin of Britain, Fragments from Lost Letters, The Penitential, Together with the Lorica of Gildas*, edited and translated by Hugh Williams, 1–252. Cymmrodorion Record Series 3. London: David Nutt, 1899.

Gregory of Nyssa. *The Life of Moses*. Translated by Abraham J. Malherbe et al., Classics of Western Spirituality. Mahwah, NJ: Paulist, 1978.

———. *The Life of St. Macrina*. In *St Gregory of Nyssa: Ascetical Works*, translated by Virginia Woods Callahan, 163–91. Fathers of the Church 58. Washington, DC: Catholic University of America Press, 1967.

———. *On Perfection*. In *St Gregory of Nyssa: Ascetical Works*, translated by Virginia Woods Callahan, 91–122. Fathers of the Church 58. Washington, DC: Catholic University of America Press, 1967.

———. *On the Making of Man*. In *Select Writings and Letters of Gregory, Bishop of Nyssa*, translated by William Moore et al., 387–427. Nicene and Post-Nicene Fathers, Ser. 2, Vol. 5. Edited by Philip Schaff et al. Grand Rapids: Eerdmans, 1976.

———. *On the Soul and the Resurrection*. Translated by Catharine P. Roth. Popular Patristic Series 12. Crestwood, NY: St. Vladimir's Seminary Press, 1993.

————. *On Virginity*. In *Select Writings and Letters of Gregory, Bishop of Nyssa*, translated by William Moore et al., 343–71. Nicene and Post-Nicene Fathers, Ser. 2, Vol. 5. Edited by Philip Schaff and Henry Wace. Grand Rapids: Eerdmans, 1976.

Gregory Palamas. *The One Hundred and Fifty Chapters: A Critical Edition, Translation and Study*. Translated by Robert E. Sinkewicz. Toronto: Pontifical Institute of Mediaeval Studies, 1988.

————. *Topics of Natural and Theological Science and on the Moral and Ascetic Life: One Hundred and Fifty Texts*. In *The Philokalia. The Complete Text Compiled by St. Nikodimos of the Holy Mountain and St. Makarios of Corinth*, Vol. 4, edited and translated by G. E. H. Palmer et al., 346–417. London: Faber and Faber, 1995.

Gregory the Great. *Dialogues*. Translated by Odo John Zimmerman. Fathers of the Church 39. Washington, DC: Catholic University of America Press, 1959.

————. *Forty Gospel Homilies*. Translated by Dom David Hurst. Kalamazoo: Cistercian, 1990.

————. *Moralia in Iob libri I–X, XI–XXII*, and *XXIII–XXXV*. Edited by Marci Adriaen. Corpus Christianorum Series Latina 143, 143A, 143B. Turnhout, Belgium: Brepols, 1979, 1985.

————. *Pastoral Care*. Translated by Henry Davis. Ancient Christian Writers 11 New York: Newman, 1950.

————. *Registrum epistolarum*. In *Patrologia cursus completes: Series latina*, vol. 77, edited by Jacques-Paul Migne, 431–1327. Paris: Migne, 1862.

Haarhoff, Theodore. *Schools of Gaul: A Study of Pagan and Christian Education in the Last Century of the Western Empire*. Oxford: Oxford University Press/Humphrey Milford, 1920.

Harkianakis, Stylianos. "Ποίηση καὶ Δόγμα εἰς τὸ ἔργο τοῦ ἁγίου Ἀνδρέου Κρήτης." In Ὁ Ἅγιος Ἀνδρέας, ἀρχιεπίσκοπος Κρήτης ὁ Ἱεροσολυμίτης, πολιοῦχος Ἐρεσοῦ Λέσβου, 316–27. Μυτιλήνη: Ἱερά Μητρόπολις Μυτιλήνης, 2005.

Heidebrecht, Doug "Distinction and Function in the Church: Reading Galatians 3:28 in Context." *Direction* 34:2 (2005) 181–93.

Heine, Ronal E. *Reading the Old Testament with the Ancient Church: Exploring the Formation of Ancient Christian Thought*. Grand Rapids: Baker Academic, 2007.

Hilary of Poitiers. *Commentary on Matthew*. Translated by D. H. William. Fathers of the Church 125. Washington, DC: Catholic University of America Press, 2012.

————. *On the Councils*. In *Hilary of Poitiers, John of Damascus*, Translated by E. W. Watson et al., 4–29. Nicene and Post-Nicene Fathers, Ser. 2, Vol. 9. Edited by Philip Schaff et al. Peabody, MA: Hendrickson, 1995.

————. *The Trinity*. Translated by Stephen McKenna. Fathers of the Church 25. Washington, DC: Catholic University of America Press, 1954.

Hofer, Andrew. "The Old Man as Christ in Justin's 'Dialogue with Trypho.'" *Vigiliae Christianae* 57.1 (2003) 1–21.

Hopko, Thomas. "Galatians 3:28: An Orthodox Interpretation." *St. Vladimir's Theological Quarterly* 35:2–3 (1991) 169–86.

Hosler, John D. "Gregory the Great's Gout: Suffering, Penitence, and Diplomacy in the Early Middle Ages." In *Where Heaven and Earth Meet: Essays on Medieval Europe in Honour of Daniel F. Callahan*, edited by Michael Frassetto et al., 11–32. Leiden: Brill, 2014.

Hunt, Hannah. *A Guide to St. Symeon the New Theologian*. Cascade Companions. Eugene, OR: Cascade, 2015.

"Icon of the Mother of God, 'Albazin' or 'The Word Was Made Flesh.'" Orthodox Church in America. https://www.oca.org/saints/lives/2042/03/09/100750-icon-of-the-mother-of-god-albazin-or-the-word-was-made-flesh.

Ignatius of Antioch. *The Epistle to Polycarp*, *The Epistle to Romans*, and *The Epistle to the Smyrnaeans*. In *Early Christian Writings*, translated by Maxwell Staniforth et al., 83–89, 99–105, 107–12. London: Penguin, 1987.

The Irish Life of Brigit. In *Celtic Spirituality*, translated by Oliver Davies et al., 140–54. The Classics of Western Spirituality 96. Mahwah, NJ: Paulist Press, 1999.

Irvin, Joseph, ed. *A Calendar of Orthodox Saints and Feast Days*. Orthodox Service Books 9. Fr. Joseph Irvin, 2019. Kindle edition.

———. *The Hours*. Orthodox Service Books 6. Fr. Joseph Irvin, 2019.

Ivanov, Sergey A. *Holy Fools in Byzantium and Beyond*. Translated by Simon Franklin. Oxford: Oxford University Press, 2006.

James, Edward. "Archaeology and the Merovingian Monastery." In *Columbanus and Merovingian Monasticism*, edited by H. B. Clarke et al., 33–55. BAR International Series 113. Oxford: British Archaeological Reports, 1981.

Jerome of Stridon. *Against the Pelagians*. In *The Principal Works of St. Jerome*, translated by W. H. Fremantle et al., 447–63. Nicene and Post-Nicene Fathers, Ser. 2, Vol. 6. Edited by Philip Schaff et al. Peabody, MA: Hendrickson, 1995.

———. *Commentary on Galatians*. Translated by Andrew Cain. Fathers of the Church 121. Washington, DC: Catholic University of America Press, 2010.

———. *Commentary on Matthew*. Translated by Thomas P. Scheck. Fathers of the Church 117. Washington, DC: Catholic University of America Press, 2008.

———. *On Illustrious Men*. Translated by Thomas P. Halton. Fathers of the Church 100. Washington, DC: Catholic University of America Press, 1955.

———. *To Eustochium* and *To Theodosius and the Other Anchorites Living in Residence with Him*. In *The Letters of St. Jerome*, translated by Charles Christopher Mierow, 28–29, 132–79. Ancient Christian Writers 33. New York: Newman, 1963.

———. *Vita beati Pauli monachi Thebaei*. In *Trois vies de Moines*, edited and translated by Edgardo M. Morales, 144–83. Sources Chrétiennes 508. Paris: Les Éditions du Cerf, 2007.

Johanny, Raymond. "Ignatius of Antioch." In *The Eucharist of the Early Christians*, edited by Willy Rordorf et al., translated by Matthew J. O'Connell, 48–70. Collegeville, MN: Liturgical, 1990.

John Cassian. *Conferences*. Translated by Colm Luibheid. New York: Paulist, 1985.

John Chrysostom. *Commentary on the Epistle to the Galatians and Homilies on the Epistle to the Ephesians*. A Library of Fathers of the Holy Catholic Church, Anterior to the Division of the East and West 5. Oxford: John Henry Parker, 1845.

———. *Homilies on Genesis 1–17*. Translated by Robert C. Hill. Fathers of the Church 74. Washington, DC: Catholic University of America Press, 1986.

John Moschus. *The Spiritual Meadow*. Translated by John Wortley. Cistercian Studies Series 139. Michigan: Cistercian, 1992.

Johnson, Dale A. *Searching for Jesus on the Silk Road*. New Sinai, 2013.

Just Jr., Arthur A. "The Apostolic Councils of Galatians and Acts: How First-Century Christians Walked Together." *CTQ* 74 (2010) 261–88.

Justin Martyr. *Dialogue with Trypho*. Translated by Thomas B. Falls et al. Edited by Michael Slusser. Selections from the Fathers of the Church 3. Washington, DC: Catholic University of America Press, 2003.

————. *The First Apology, The Second Apology, Dialogue with Trypho, Exhortation to the Greeks, Discourse to the Greeks, The Monarchy or The Rule of God*. Translated by Thomas B. Falls. Fathers of the Church 6. Washington, DC: Catholic University of America Press, 1965.

————.᾿Ιουστίνου ἀπολογία ὑπὲρ Χριστιανῶν πρὸς Ἀντωνίνον τὸν Εὐσεβῆ and [*Pars Secunda*] τοῦ αὐτοῦ ἁγίου ᾿Ιουστίνου φιλοσόφου καὶ μάρτυρος ἀπολογία ὑπὲρ Χριστιανῶν πρὸς τὴν Ῥωμαίων σύγκλητον A. In *Justin, Philosopher and Martyr: Apologies*, edited and translated by Denis Minns et al., 80–323. Oxford: Oxford University Press, 2009.

Kelly, J. N. D. *Golden Mouth: The Story of John Chrysostom—Ascetic, Preacher, Bishop*. Ithaca, NY: Cornell University Press, 1995.

Kesich, Veselin. *Formation and Struggles: The Birth of the Church AD 33–200*. Crestwood, NY: St. Vladimir's Seminary Press, 2007.

Keynes, Simon. "Æthelbald." In *The Wiley Blackwell Encyclopedia of Anglo-Saxon England*, 2nd ed., edited by Michael Lapidge et al., 13–14. West Sussex, UK: Wiley Blackwell, 2014.

Laird, Martin "Darkness." In *The Brill Dictionary of St Gregory of Nyssa*, edited by Lucas Francisco Mateo-Seco et al., translated by Seth Cherney, 203–5. Leiden: Brill, 2010.

Lapidge, Michael. "Bede's Metrical Vita S. Cuthberti." In *St Cuthbert, His Cult and His Community to A.D. 1200*, edited by Gerald Bonner et al., 77–93. Woodbridge, UK: Boydell, 1995.

Lawrence, C. H. *Medieval Monasticism: Forms of Religious Life in Western Europe in the Middle Ages*. Oxon, UK: Routledge, 2015.

Lawson, Russell N. *Science in the Ancient World: From Antiquity Through the Middle Ages*. Santa Barbara, CA: ABC-CLIO, 2021.

Lee, John A. L. "Why Didn't St Basil Write in New Testament Greek?" *Phronema* 25 (2010) 3–20.

The Letter of Cuthbert to Cuthwin. In *A History of the English Church and People*, translated by Leo Sherley-Price, 18–20. Harmondsworth, Middlesex: Penguin, 1955.

Liddell, Henry George, et al. *A Greek-English Lexicon*. 9th ed. Oxford: Clarendon, 1996.

The Life of St. Brigit the Virgin by Cogitosus. In *Celtic Spirituality*, translated by Oliver Davies et al., 122–39. The Classics of Western Spirituality 96. Mahwah, NJ: Paulist, 1999.

Louth, Andrew. "Gregory the Great in the Byzantine Tradition." In *A Companion to Gregory the Great*, edited by Bronwen Neil et al., 343–58. Brill's Companions to the Christian Tradition 47. Leiden: Brill, 2013.

————. "Recent Research on St Maximus the Confessor: A Survey." *St Vladimir's Theological Quarterly* 42:1 (1998) 67–84.

Love, Rosalind. "The World of Latin Learning." In *The Cambridge Companion to Bede*, edited by Scott DeGregorio, 40–53. Cambridge, UK: Cambridge University Press, 2010.

Maraval, Pierre. "Biography of Gregory of Nyssa." In *The Brill Dictionary of Gregory of Nyssa*, edited by Lucas Francisco Mateo-Seco et al., translated by Seth Cherney, 103–16. Supplements to Vigiliae Christianae 99. Leiden: Brill, 2010.

The Martyrdom of Polycarp. In *Early Christian Writings*, translated by Maxwell Staniforth et al., 125–35. London: Penguin, 1987.

Mathisen, Ralph W. "Bishops, Barbarians, and the 'Dark Ages': The Fate of Late Roman Educational Institutions in Late Antique Gaul." In *Medieval Education*, edited by Ronald B. Begley et al., 1–27. New York: Fordham University Press, 2005.

Maximus the Confessor. *Four Hundred Texts on Love*. In *The Philokalia. The Complete Text Complied by St Nikodimos of the Holy Mountain and St Makarios of Corinth*, Vol. 2, edited and translated by G. E. H. Palmer et al., 52–113. London: Faber and Faber, 1981.

———. *Letter 2: On Love*. In *Maximus the Confessor*, edited and translated by Andrew Louth, 84–93. London: Routledge, 1996.

McCulloh, John M. "Confessor Saints and the Origins of Monasticism: The *Lives* of Saints Antony and Martin." In *The Middle Ages in Texts and Texture: Reflections on Medieval Sources*, edited by Jason Glenn, 21–32. University of Toronto Press, 2011.

McGuckin, John A. "Aliens and Citizens of Elsewhere: *Xeniteia* in East Christian Monastic Literature." In *Strangers to Themselves: The Byzantine Outsider, Papers from the Thirty-second Spring Symposium of Byzantine Studies, University of Sussex, Brighton, March 1998*, edited by Dion C. Smythe, 23–38. Oxon, UK: Routledge, 2016.

———. "China, Autonomous Orthodox Church of." In *The Encyclopedia of Eastern Orthodox Christianity, Vol. 1: A–M*, edited by John Anthony McGuckin, 112–14. Chichester, West Sussex: Blackwell Publishing, 2011.

———. *The Orthodox Church: An Introduction to Its History, Doctrine, and Spiritual Culture*. Malden, MA: Blackwell, 2008.

———. *St. Cyril of Alexandria. The Christological Controversy: Its History, Theology, and Texts*. Supplements to Vigiliae Christianae 23. Leiden: Brill, 1994.

McLees, Nectaria. "The Marvelous Life of Patriarch Sophronius I, His Company of Saints, and the Fall of Byzantine Jerusalem." *Road to Emmaus* 43 (2010) 47–67.

McSherry, James. *Outreach and Renewal: A First-Millennium Legacy for the Third-Millennium Church*. Cistercian Studies Series 236. Trappist, KY: Cistercian, 2011.

Meek, Donald E. *The Quest for Celtic Christianity*. Boat of Garten, Scotland: Handsel, 2000.

Mertens, Andre. *The Old English Lives of St Martin of Tours: Edition and Study*. Universitätsverlag Göttingen, 2017.

Meyendorff, John. *Byzantine Theology: Historical Trends and Doctrinal Themes*. New York: Fordham University Press, 1974.

———. *St. Gregory Palamas and Orthodox Spirituality*. Translated by Adele Fisk. Crestwood, NY: St Vladimir's Seminary Press, 1974.

Nasuti, Harry P. *Defining the Sacred Songs: Genre, Tradition and the Post-Critical Interpretation of the Psalms*. Sheffield Academic, 1999.

Nichols, Aidan. *Byzantine Gospel: Maximus the Confessor in Modern Scholarship*. Eugene, OR: Wipf and Stock Publishers, 1993.

Niketas Stethatos. *The Life of Saint Symeon the New Theologian*. Translated by Richard P. H. Greenfield. Dumbarton Oaks Medieval Library 20. Cambridge, MA: Harvard University Press, 2013.

Novum Testamentum Graece. 28th ed. Edited by the Institute for New Testament Textual Research Münster/Westphalia under the direction of Holger Strutwolf. Stuttgart: Deutsche Bibelgesellschaft, 2012.

O'Keefe, John J. "Christianizing Malachi: Fifth-Century Insights from Cyril of Alexandria." *Vigiliae Christianae* 50:2 (1996) 136–58.

O'Loughlin, Thomas. *Celtic Theology: Humanity, World and God in Early Irish Writings*. London: Continuum, 2000.

The Orthodox Study Bible. St. Athanasius Academy of Orthodox Theology. Nashville: Thomas Nelson, 2008.

Our Thoughts Determine Our Lives: The Life and Teachings of Elder Thaddeus of Vitovnica. Translated by Ana Smiljanic. Platina, CA: Saint Herman of Alaska Brotherhood, 2015.

Paffhausen, Jonah. "Natural Contemplation in St. Maximus the Confessor and St. Isaac the Syrian." In *Toward an Ecology of Transfiguration: Orthodox Christian Perspectives on Environment, Nature, and Creation*, edited by John Chryssavgis et al., 46–58. New York: Fordham University Press, 2013.

Patrick's Declaration of the Great Works of God. In *Celtic Spirituality*, translated by Oliver Davies et al., 67–83. The Classics of Western Spirituality 96. Mahwah, NJ: Paulist, 1999.

Paul the Deacon. *Sancti Gregorii Magni Vita.* In *Patrologia cursus completes: Series latina*, vol. 75, edited by Jacques-Paul Migne, 41A–242B. Paris: Migne, 1862.

Paulinus. *Life of St. Ambrose.* Translated by John A. Lacy. In *Early Christian Biographies*, edited by Roy J. Deferrari, 25–66. Fathers of the Church 15. Washington, DC: Catholic University of America Press, 1952.

Penella, Robert J. "The Progymnasmata in Imperial Greek Education." *Classical World* 105:1 (2011) 77–90.

Photios the Great. *The Mystagogy of the Holy Spirit.* Translated by Joseph P. Farrell. Brookline, MA: Holy Cross Orthodox Press, 1987.

Plested, Marcus. "The Ascetic Tradition." In *The Oxford Handbook of Maximus the Confessor*, edited by Pauline Allen et al., 164–76. Oxford: Oxford University Press, 2015.

Pliny the Younger. *Complete Letters.* Translated by P. G. Walsh. Oxford: Oxford University Press, 2006.

Polycarp of Smyrna. *The Epistle of Polycarp to the Philippians.* In *Early Christian Writings*, translated by Maxwell Staniforth et al., 119–24. London: Penguin, 1987.

Relatio motionis. In *Maximus the Confessor and His Companions: Documents from Exile*, edited and translated by Pauline Allen and Bronwen Neil, 48–74. Oxford: Oxford University Press, 2002.

Rhee, Helen. *Early Christian Literature: Christ and Culture in the Second and Third Centuries.* Abingdon, Oxon, UK: Routledge, 2005.

Ricci, Cristina. "Gregory's Missions to the Barbarians." In *A Companion to Gregory the Great*, edited by Bronwen Neil et al., 47–56. Brill's Companions to the Christian Tradition 47. Leiden: Brill, 2013.

Russell, Norman. *The Doctrine of Deification in the Greek Patristic Tradition.* Oxford: Oxford University Press, 2004.

———. *Gregory Palamas and the Making of Palamism in the Modern Age.* Oxford: Oxford University Press, 2019.

Russell, Paul S. *Making Your Life a Christian Life.* Bloomington, IN: AuthorHouse, 2009.

Saint Mary of Egypt: Three Medieval Lives in Verse. Translated by Ronald E. Pepin and Hugh Feiss. Cistercian Studies Series 209. Michigan: Cistercian, 2005.

The Sayings of the Desert Fathers: The Alphabetical Collection. Translated by Benedicta Ward. Cistercian Studies Series 59. Michigan: Cistercian, 1975.

Serapion of Thmuis: Against the Manicheans and Pastoral Letters. Translated by Oliver Herbel. Early Christian Studies 14. Strathfield, New South Wales, Australia: St Pauls, 2011.

Siemens, James. *The Christology of Theodore of Tarsus: The* Laterculus Malalianus *and the Person and Work of Christ*. Studia Traditionis Theologiae: Explorations in Early and Medieval Theology 6. Turnhout: Brepols, 2010.

Simonetti, Manlio. "Exegesis." In *The Brill Dictionary of St Gregory of Nyssa*, edited by Lucas Francisco Mateo-Seco and Giulio Maspero, translated by Seth Cherney, 331–38. Leiden: Brill, 2010.

———. "Vit Moys, De vita Moysis." In *The Brill Dictionary of St Gregory of Nyssa*, edited by Lucas Francisco Mateo-Seco et al., translated by Seth Cherney, 788–90. Leiden: Brill, 2010.

Siniossoglou, Niketas. *Radical Platonism in Byzantium: Illumination and Utopia and Gemistos Plethon*. Cambridge, UK: Cambridge University Press, 2011.

The Sixth Ecumenical Council—The Third Council of Constantinople, A.D. 680–681. In *The Seven Ecumenical Councils of the Undivided Church*, translated by Henry R. Percival, 325–53. Nicene and Post-Nicene Fathers, Ser. 2, Vol. 14. Edited by Philip Schaff et al. Peabody, MA: Hendrickson, 1995.

Sophronius of Jerusalem. *The Life of Saint Mary of Egypt*. In *The Great Canon of Saint Andrew of Crete and The Life of Saint Mary of Egypt*, edited and translated by Mother Thekla et al., 100–38. Finnian, 2013.

———. *Sophronius of Jerusalem and Seventh-Century Heresy: The Synodical Letter and Other Documents*. Edited by Pauline Allen. Oxford: Oxford University Press, 2009.

Sozomen. Ἐκκλησιαστικὴ ἱστορία. In *Histoire ecclésiastique, Livres iii–iv*. Edited by J. Bidez. Translated by André-Jean Festugière. Sources Chrétiennes 418. Paris, Les Éditions du Cerf, 1996.

Stancliffe, Clare. "The Irish Tradition in Northumbria After the Synod of Whitby." In *The Lindisfarne Gospels: New Perspectives*, edited by Richard Gameson, 19–42. Leiden: Brill, 2017.

———. "Red, White and Blue Martyrdom." In *Ireland in Early Medieval Europe: Studies in Memory of Kathleen Hughes*, edited by Dorothy Whitelock et al., 21–46. Cambridge, UK: Cambridge University Press, 1982.

———. *St. Martin and His Hagiographer: History and Miracle in Sulpicius Severus*. Oxford: Oxford University Press, 1983.

Stylianopoulos, Theodore G. *The New Testament: An Orthodox Perspective*, vol. 1: *Scripture, Tradition, Hermeneutics*. Brookline, MA: Holy Cross Orthodox Press, 1997.

Sulpicius Severus. *Chronicorum*. In *Chroniques*. Edited by Ghislaine de Senneville-Grave. Sources Chrétiennes 441. Paris, Les Éditions du Cerf, 1999.

———. *Epistula prima, ad Eusebium, Epistula secunda, ad Aurelium diaconum*, and *Epistula tertia, Sulpicius Severus Bassulae parenti venerabili salutem* In *Vie de Saint Martin, Tome 1*, edited and translated by Jacques Fontaine, 316–45. Sources Chrétiennes 133. Paris, Les Éditions du Cerf, 1967.

———. *Gallus sive Dialogi de virtutibus sancti Martini*. In *Gallus: Dialogues sur les «vertus» de saint Martin*. Edited and translated by Jacques Fontaine et al. Sources Chrétiennes 510. Paris: Les Éditions du Cerf, 2006.

———. *Sulpicius Severus: The Complete Works*. Translated by Richard J. Goodrich. NY, NJ: Newman, 2015.

———. *Sulpicius Severus: Writings*. Translated by Bernard M. Peebles. In *The Fathers of the Church*, Volume 7. Washington, DC: Catholic University of America Press, 1947.

———. *Vita Sancti Martini episcopi*. In *Sulpicius Severus' Vita Martini*, edited and translated by Philip Burton, 94–129. Oxford: Oxford University Press, 2017.

"Sunday of St. Mary of Egypt." Greek Orthodox Archdiocese of America. https://www. goarch.org/sunday-stmaryofegypt.

Symeon the New Theologian. *The Discourses.* Translated by C. J. De Catanzaro. Introduction by George Maloney. Classics of Western Spirituality. Mahwah, NJ: Paulist, 1980.

———. *The Epistles of St. Symeon the New Theologian.* Translated by H. J. M. Turner. Oxford Early Christian Texts. Oxford: Oxford University Press, 2009.

Tatakis, Basil N. *Christian Philosophy in the Patristic and Byzantine Tradition.* Edited and translated by George Dion. Dragas. Rollinsford, NH: Orthodox Research Institute, 2007.

Tertullian. *Apology.* In *Latin Christianity: Its Founder, Tertullian. Three Parts: I. Apologetic; II. Anti-Marcion; III. Ethical,* translated by S. Thelwall, 17–55. Ante-Nicene Fathers 3. Edited by Alexander Roberts et al. Peabody, MA: Hendrickson, 1994.

Tornau, Christian. "Intertextuality in Early Latin Hagiography: Sulpicius Severus and the *Vita Antonii.*" In *Studia Patristica, Vol. XXXV,* edited by M. F. Wiles et al., 158–66. Leuven: Peeters, 2001.

Two Lives of Saint Cuthbert. Edited and translated by Bertram Colgrave. Cambridge, UK: Cambridge University Press, 1940.

Uzukwu, Gesila Nneka. "Gal 3,28 and Its Alleged Relationship to Rabbinic Writings." *Biblica* 91:3 (2010) 370–92.

Verba Seniorum (Apophthegmata Patrum, Collectio Latina Systematica). In *Patrologia cursus completes: Series latina,* vol. *73,* edited by Jacques-Paul Migne, 855–1062. Paris: Migne, 1849.

Vita Sancti Cuthberti Auctore Anonymo. In *Two Lives of Saint Cuthbert.* Edited and translated by Bertram Colgrave. Cambridge, UK: Cambridge University Press, 1940.

The Voyage of Brendan. In *Celtic Spirituality,* translated by Oliver Davies et al., 155–90. The Classics of Western Spirituality 96. Mahwah, NJ: Paulist, 1999.

Ware, Kallistos. *The Orthodox Way.* Crestwood, NY: St. Vladimir's Seminary Press, 1986.

———. "St. Nikodimos and the Philokalia." In *The Philokalia: A Classic Text of Orthodox Spirituality,* edited by Brock Bingaman et al., 9–35. Oxford: Oxford University Press, 2012.

Weinandy, Thomas G., and Daniel A. Keating. *Athanasius and His Legacy: Trinitarian-Incarnation Soteriology and Its Reception.* Minneapolis, MN: Fortress, 2017.

Wessel, Susan. "The Theology of Agape in Maximus the Confessor." *St Vladimir's Theological Quarterly* 55:3 (2011) 319–42.

Wooding, Jonathan M., et al., eds. *Adomnán of Iona: Theologian, Lawmaker, Peacemaker.* Dublin: Four Courts, 2010.

Woods, Richard. "Ireland: History." In *Encyclopedia of Monasticism,* edited by William M. Johnston et al., 657–61. London: Routledge, 2000.

Yaokum, Ioasaph, and Ioannis Chen (Interviewees). "Beyond the Great Wall: Orthodoxy in China." *Road to Emmaus* 4:2 (2003) 3–48.